When the World [...] in the Teeth

How to Get Back Up Again

By Anita Brown

I dedicate this book to my wonderful family, friends and all those who have helped me along the way in this journey of self discovery.

Thank you I could not have done it without you.

Contents

Introduction

Chapter 1   I'm Fine

Chapter 2   Letting Go

Chapter 3   The Financial Titanic

Chapter 4   Wants and Needs

Chapter 5   Twenty Tips to Cut Costs

Chapter 6   A New Start?

Chapter 7   Where am I? Fighting the Overwhelm

Chapter 8   The Discard

Chapter 9   Who is in My Corner?

Chapter 10   The Aftermath

Chapter 11   Understanding the Warning Signs

Chapter 12   What the F***!

Chapter 13   Mind Over Matter

Chapter 14   Happy New Year

Chapter 15   How to Recover from a Toxic Encounter

Chapter 16   Putting Myself First

Chapter 17   Dark Night of the Soul

Chapter 18   Finding Support

Chapter 19   Edna

Chapter 20   Me, Myself and I

Chapter 21   The Golden Nugget

Chapter 22   Climbing the Mountain

Chapter 23   Tea with a Psychopath

Chapter 24   Who Bluffs Best Survives

Chapter 25   Trust Your Gut

Chapter 26   Psychopathic Hangover

Chapter 27   Happy Ever After

Acknowledgements

This book is not intended to be a substitute for the medical advice of a licensed physician. The reader should consult with their doctor in any matters relating to his or her health.

The information contained within this eBook is strictly for educational purposes. If you wish to apply ideas contained in this eBook, you are taking full responsibility for your actions.

The methods described within this eBook are the author's personal thoughts. They are not intended to be a definitive set of instructions. You may discover that there are other methods and materials to accomplish the same end result. While the author has made every effort to ensure the accuracy of the information within this book, the author does not assume and hereby disclaims any liability to any party for any loss, damage, or disruption caused by errors or omissions, whether such errors or omissions result from accident, negligence, or any other cause.

No part of this eBook may be reproduced or transmitted in any form or by any means, electronic or mechanical, including photocopying, recording or by any information storage and retrieval system, without written permission from the author.

Cover Photograph provided by Nick Demou from Pexels

© October 2016 Anita Brown

Introduction

If you are reading this introduction, then the chances are either you or someone you know is facing a tough time. Maybe you were attracted by the title or the cover, or maybe this book has attracted your attention for a yet unknown reason. Maybe you came across this book by accident, or someone gave it to you. Maybe you are meant to share something within its pages with someone close to you, or a complete stranger. If so you are here for a reason and if it is not you who needs help please, be the conduit for someone else who needs it.

There could be a million and one different problems that you are facing and I don't hope to be able to cover them all, or to understand exactly how you feel right now, however what I am going to say to you is that you are not alone. This is just a dip in the road we call life and just as a road goes down it also goes up. Focusing on the dip robs you of the ability to see the view from the top of the hill.

Sometimes in life our hardest challenges appear when we feel that we have no one to share them with. We are hurting and angry, blaming whomever or whatever we can. Screaming out "Why me?" We may be surrounded by people, but feel unable to communicate how lost and alone we feel, and the more we can't communicate the worse we feel. So the downward spiral continues.....

Here is a message just for you as you face your darkest hour.

"I want you to imagine feeling right now that sense of letting go, as I wrap my arms around you in a big hug, because that is exactly what I am imagining. This hug is just for you and no-one else. Feel its warmth and the gentle pressure, as you rest your head on my shoulder. Whatever you are experiencing, you can get through this and I am here to hold your hand, and guide you through until you get there. I will never judge you and will love you unconditionally, as I know that deep down you want to be the best you can be, and share your love with the world no matter what challenges you are currently facing.

We will walk the road together however fast or slow you need to go. During every tough moment I will be standing cheering you on from the sidelines, and soon the troubles you are experiencing will be nothing but a fading memory. I will always be there for you to turn to.

I will protect you from harm and guide you in making choices that will be better for you. I will teach you to trust again and believe in the wonder of you.

However to accomplish this task I need to ask something of you in return. I want you to promise with all of your heart that you will try, and even if you stumble a bit, I want you to keep coming back. I want you to truly listen and trust that things can be different. I want you to give me the chance to work that miracle in your life.

Can you do that?

Can you try?

Yes.........?

Good then hold my hand as we walk the road together.

Lots of Love

From

Your Positive Self

Chapter 1

I'm Fine

I opened my eyes blearily and peered out of the dusty window. The sun shone brightly, tall weeds swayed in the gentle breeze and the trill sound of happy birds resounded in my ears. Everything outside looked bright and hopeful, but in the pit of my van, hope was the last thing that I wanted to face.

It was the eighteenth of April, my fortieth birthday and, like many people, it's on days like this that you take stock of your life. Truly face where you are and what you haven't got. I was forty living in the back of a dark blue combi-van. I had no money to support my camera shop due in part to the recession, my kids had moved to live with my ex-husband when I'd lost my home and it was only a matter of time before everything else collapsed. My failing business loomed ominously as I was parked in the parking space behind it. The sensation of being strapped in a runaway rollercoaster, that was doomed to crash in carnage and flames, flashed through my mind. The end was inevitable there was no escape.

I shifted uncomfortably in my sleeping bag, becoming aware of my sore back and groaned miserably. My feet were still blocks of ice and I had the starting of a cramp in my leg, from sleeping in a space that was half a foot too short for my height. Propelled by the forthcoming pain of not moving, I clambered wearily out of my sleeping bag, and fumbled for some clothes. Restful sleep was a distant memory as I was unable to park until long after everyone was asleep, for fear of being moved on. Even then I slept on constant alert listening in case anyone thought it was a good idea to attack a woman, sleeping alone in her van.

I felt unkempt and in need of a shower, but there wasn't much I could do about that at the moment. Finally after banging my head and elbows numerous times in the cramped space, I emerged clumsily dressed, from the back of my van.

Sitting on the now pleasantly warm bonnet, I surveyed the supermarket carrier bag of food that I had purchased the night before, with the last few coins in my pocket. A tired dodgy looking sandwich, probably not a good idea, and a half eaten chocolate bar was all that was left. I reached for the chocolate. Chocolate was what I needed.

Sounds of people awakening in the flats above the shops, filtered down to me. I waved and smiled at a couple on the balcony, and tried to look like I had just arrived for work. I was hoping they didn't realise I had actually been there all night. I could hear people laughing and joking, Bon Jovi played on the radio, the sound of water running, and the smell of bacon frying in a pan. My stomach grumbled loudly in protest.

I felt like life was going on without me, and I was trapped looking in on a world that I was no longer a part of. My mask of "I'm fine" finally slipped, smashed to pieces on the floor.

Suddenly I felt very, very alone.

Chapter 2
Letting Go

There comes a time in everyone's life when bad stuff just happens, and we have all experienced times when we are feeling down for a while. But what happens if that for a while keeps on going, and there is no end in sight? No matter what you are facing if you weren't continuing to have an emotional response to it, then it wouldn't be such a big problem for you. So whether it is relationship issues, an illness, financial issues or a bully, by changing the way we think and feel about it, we can ultimately change how it affects us. But aren't we emotional beings constantly at the mercy of our thoughts? Or are we?

Often when we feel like we can't take anymore, it is because we are in what I affectionately like to call, "overwhelm". Overwhelm is where we are frantically looking around for a quick fix or a way to block out the pain. It is a state of mind where you have constant repetitive thoughts, high levels of stress, are quick to anger, or burst into tears and have a constant feeling of there is just too much to cope with and I don't want to do this anymore, or I want to escape.

As human beings we are programmed to either seek pleasure or to go to great lengths to avoid pain. When we are forced into a situation which requires us to embrace the emotions of pain as well, we often avoid it rather than face it, regardless of the consequences for ourselves, or those around us.

Admitting to ourselves that we are not coping is a massive challenge because it means letting go of the outcome, and we can't let go can we. We have invested too much in it. We want someone to fix it for us so we don't have to look too closely, but we won't let go so nothing works. The fear of losing our control is terrifying, and we would do anything rather than face that, even if it means digging a deeper hole of despair to hide in.

So let us just move past that particular challenge as quickly as possible shall we. You picked up this book because there was some area of your life that you're not coping with, and I can already hear the chorus of inner voices, "No I'm fine". I will make it a little easier for you. I started writing this book originally, because I wasn't coping. I spent years with the default "I'm fine" tattooed across my forehead. The day I finally looked at myself in the mirror and admitted to myself I wasn't coping, was the day a huge weight was lifted from my shoulders, a line so to speak in the sand, a starting point for self realization. Now it is your turn to draw that line in the sand. You didn't choose this book because I am some famous celebrity, or guru, that you just had to read about, because I'm not. I am just an ordinary woman from Essex, UK, an average everyday person just like you. The reason you chose this book is because it spoke to you on an unconscious level, because you are ready to move forward with your life. You are ready to admit to yourself that on some level you're not coping.

Ok then hands up who isn't coping...

Good that is all of us then

In order for us to move forward, we have to choose between being an ostrich or a meerkat. Both face the same challenge, but one will bury his head in the sand so he can't see what is coming, and the other seeks help, works as a team and faces things head on.

Look at it like you have a festering wound as a child covered by a dirty plaster. Now you know that grabbing hold of the plaster and ripping it off is going to sting, and you so don't want to feel that pain, so you shove another plaster over the top to contain the pus and ignore it. But it hurts like hell and you know it is getting more infected, because your skin feels hot and swollen, and it hurts even more now, and it is leaking out the side of the dressing. People ask you about it and you say it is fine, and you hide it away from sight. You don't like lying but if you rip off the plaster now it will hurt even worse than before. Won't it? You will also get into trouble with your parents for not saying anything about it. So you leave it alone and hope it goes away, and keep adding bigger plasters until you absolutely have to deal with it, and then you are left with an unsightly scar. Emotional wounds are exactly the same.

Most people stay locked into difficult situations hiding from the truth, scared in case it hurts more to leave than to stay. This could be a traumatic event, an abusive situation, a business, a financial loss, a friendship, a marriage or a health condition it doesn't matter. You have deliberately covered up the problem by continually pouring more and more of your time, emotions, and identity, your money, hopes and dreams into this and letting go just doesn't seem possible. What would I be, how would I cope, what would happen, why did this happen and what was the point of it all? So we keep on adding plasters to our wound.

Often we fail to see it wasn't the thing at the end that was important, but the journey we take. It is the lessons we learn along the way in getting to know ourselves and understanding our place in the world. So you didn't avoid being hurt, have a successful business, or have the marriage of your dreams, have a perfect family, get that grade, or be the most popular person in school this time. It doesn't mean you never will. Bad stuff just happens and sometimes that is how we learn. If you never let go of your investment in the past, and keep on investing in the past you won't have the ability to invest in the future, and make your dreams come true.

A very simple example of this is when I spoke to a lovely lady a few years back. She owned a very beautiful shop packed full of crystals and handmade items. In the middle of the shop was an amazing full size papier mache tree that reached up to the ceiling of the shop. It was a truly amazing fixture for the shop and the lady used it to her advantage to display her wares. She looked a little sad so I asked her why and she told me she had a great opportunity to move abroad to expand her business, but she had to get rid of the shop. She desperately wanted to pass on the handmade tree to the next owner, but no one was interested in taking on the shop with the tree still in situ. They wanted it taken down. She talked to me of all the effort and time she had put into creating it, and all the memories associated with it. She was literally putting her new life opportunities on hold waiting for someone who would want the tree, because she couldn't let go.

I asked her what the tree was made of, paint, paper, glitter and wood. Alone they were only materials. The real magic was in the creation. The emotions associated with the construction frustration, pain, awe, happiness. The pride when it was finished. The many glowing comments she received from her customers. So I asked her was not the journey of making it, learning from it, and sharing it more important than the finished product. She smiled and nodded understanding my reference.

Her need to have the tree go to a good home was just her need for validation that all her effort had produced something, a product something in the physical, proof that it had been worthwhile. But our most valuable lessons aren't found in the physical they are found in the spiritual growth we experience. Often we want things finished off. Tied up with a big red bow before we can move forward, but life doesn't often allow that to happen. Like wanting your ex to admit he made a mistake in leaving you so you can reject them first. For your employer to give you a raise and a better job after all your hard work. For your so called friend to acknowledge that you are her best friend, after all the effort you made even though she still treats you badly. For your Mum to tell you that she loves you even though she has never shown any interest in you. Life is not interested in an end before a beginning. It flows very much like the branches of a tree. A fork in the road that appears for you take a different path, but if you don't take that fork because you are trying to tidy things up with a big red bow, you will miss the next opportunity life has for you.

So there we all are desperately clinging to our own branch, looking in terror at the next fork.

Chapter 3

The Financial Titanic

Naively I believed that the worst had happened, but I was to be sorely wrong. Life became a constant battle. I was working insane hours bookkeeping or working in the camera shop, and spending every penny I earned on the debts of my shop. Tiredness was a constant companion. Days, blended into nights. Weeks, blended into weekends. I worked until I fell asleep and often I did with my head propped up against the computer screen. I felt totally alone and unable to communicate, I was so tired I was on auto-pilot.

I was desperate to find a way to extract myself from this mess, but like the Titanic I was going down with the anchor wrapped firmly around my ankles. Dragging me down into the depths I could almost feel the water closing over my head as I struggled for breath.

However to the outside world I was still pretending. Occasionally friends would ask how I was doing and I would give the perfunctory answer that I was fine. Anything more in depth and I would make an excuse, and leave the conversation. The only person who I confided in a little was my then, on and off boyfriend, the man I naively looked up to and believed in. But even then the need to be good enough in his eyes was my constant demon. I needed him to tell me that everything would be ok, but gradually as I became more and more desperate for his attention he became more and more distant. Previously he had been so encouraging at my purchase of the shop, posing for the joint publicity shots, welcoming customers into the shop, but now he rapidly lost interest as my money ran out. Suddenly rugby and drinking with his friends became more important and I didn't have the energy to question why. Everyone I think by now knew I was going to crash and burn and he must have done too. Maybe he didn't want to watch me crash, didn't want the responsibility, or preferred the head in the sand option, or he just didn't care, but it made me angry that he had jumped in the lifeboat and left me to sink. His life revolved around social interaction with a multitude of girly friends and mine wasn't. He was constantly busy other than the late night booty call. Eventually I didn't want to go out and do the happy face and pretend I was ok anymore. So I didn't even notice he wasn't asking me to go, and even if I had I wouldn't have questioned it.

Nothing quite prepares you for life on the streets. The first few days had been ok as though I was camping but soon it became more difficult. I hadn't intended it to be for longer than a few weeks, but as the days became weeks and then became months, it became clear I was trapped. My boyfriend was keen to keep our relationship on a very non-serious footing as he was living with his sister and her partner. Now I look back and I can't understand why I didn't notice how little he cared for me if he was happy for me to sleep in my van for most of the week, and only popping to his for the odd night. However I strangely was grateful for those odd nights where I had a real bed and a shower. I was still firmly in denial and the only thing I had left was my misplaced pride, and I clung to that with grim death-grip determination. I was always fine but even I could see the uncomfortable expressions on people's faces when they found out my situation. I stopped talking and withdrew even more. People felt awkward around me and I avoided them as much as possible. I didn't want anyone's help it was my fault and I would sort it out. I felt I deserved to suffer for having to as I saw it abandon my kids to my ex-husband, and buying into a failed business. I was in a pool of self hatred and loathing and I was the only one who had a ticket.

While at work being a mobile bookkeeper I arrived in a suit with the van carefully hidden out of view. No-one realised how bad it was. I was leading a bizarre double life of hobo and executive. The most everyday things that people take for granted became a big deal for me. A toilet, shower and a washing machine were big problems that previously I hadn't even thought of.

Tesco's became my port of call. Every morning first thing I drove down there and used their facilities for a quick wash with hot water and brushing of my teeth. A "shower" was achieved by standing in a washing up bowl with a jug in the shop, hidden from view of the shop window by a thin curtain on a Sunday. To be honest it was so embarrassing that it was actually funny. Trying your best not to fall out of the washing up bowl, wet and soapy into public view was just so comical.

One of the hardest things I found to deal with is that you have nowhere to go. Sounds strange, doesn't it, but everyone goes to work and comes home and flops in front of the television, but imagine not being able to do that. Being confined to sitting in the front seat of your van, knowing you can't park anywhere for long, but not wanting to waste diesel driving around in circles. You just can't fully relax. My life consisted of moving around trying to find somewhere to just be. My clothing looked crumpled, and I looked like I was sleeping in my van which meant I felt even worse about being around people.

I cut back on absolutely everything and by October I had managed to save enough money that I could finally move from my van into an old hotel room. Finally I was off the streets and had my own bed. Unless you have lived on the streets you cannot imagine the pure bliss of having a toilet and a shower. The first week I was there I just walked into the shower and cried. Just the ability to be properly clean and to be able to use the toilet at 4am was astounding to me. I didn't care about anything else, I just felt the richest person in the world.

The first Christmas period had arrived and so unfortunately had the snow. The worst winter for thirty years battered the shop. Snow drifts and ice were everywhere. Temperatures plummeted and the heating couldn't cope. It was often colder in the shop than it was outside. We had taken to wearing our coats indoors, in an effort to keep warm and invested in some electric fires, which saw the electric bill go through the roof. Customers put off by the horrendous weather chose to shop from home, or go to the town centre. Roads were hazardous and the pavements were awful. Many of the customers were older and chose to just stay at home. The Christmas sales injection of cash failed to materialise, and was quickly followed by an even harsher January with constant staff illnesses, no doubt made worse, by the lack of warmth in the shop. Eventually I had been forced to close the shop for a few days as no-one was well enough to work.

By the time the winter was over it was clear that financially I still wasn't doing well. The recession had got worse and was showing no signs of ending. People were cutting back on spending, and if they did spend it was on essentials not camera equipment. I had had to reduce the amount of time the shop was open as I couldn't afford the staff to be there full time, and with my part-time bookkeeping job being mobile I couldn't be there either. So I shut on the worst days of the week and focused on making the other days even better.

Supermarkets became my biggest competitors often selling cameras for less than I could buy them wholesale. I lost count of the times that I would spend time with a potential customer, only for them to buy an import or get it from a supermarket. I can still remember standing in Tesco's with an almost irresistible urge to rant and rave at passing customers about the injustice of the big supermarkets, wading into a market they were never in before, and crushing the little independent retailer. But I had said nothing, buried the panic and worked harder supplementing the short fall in income from the shop, with the income from my bookkeeping. It had to end soon. Things had to pick up. I just had to survive till then and that is what I had concentrated on. Just one day at a time.

Finally winter came to an end, but with spring came the rain, and it was at this point that it became apparent that the shop had a big leaking problem that originated from the gutter above the front window. Pigeons had caused massive structural damage and the result was I arrived to find all my front window display cases swimming in dirty smelly brown water, which contained not only pigeon pooh, but also the putrefied remains of more than one bird that had died in the gutter.

I was liable for half the repairs required which would run into thousands of pounds. So I had been forced to remove all my products from the window every night to prevent them being damaged, and use buckets and trays to catch the water during the day. I even had one of my staff who would keep a watch out for any birds and run out with a pigeon pole to scare them away in case they added to the problem.

This hadn't helped the perception that we were a thriving business even with notices on the door that we were open for business. Many customers commented that they thought the shop had moved away as there was no stock in the window.

During this time the council decided in their wisdom to renovate the pavements outside the shop, which included cordoning off the parking spaces which the few customers left relied on. So now the ability to have customers drop in was seriously hampered by them having to walk a fair distance from where ever they managed to find a parking space. One by one the shops around me started to close down. I had often sat looking through the empty display cases and out the front windows at the traffic driving by separated from me by an army of unmanned workmen's barriers. Noticing absent-mindedly the constant dripping and plopping sounds of water hitting the buckets around and the ever present stench of pigeon pooh.

Eventually by a stroke of luck the landlord who held my lease for the shop took pity on me, and let me out of my seven year contract early. I would lose my deposit but I could stop paying the huge monthly rent. I surveyed the shop. I still had a lot of fixtures and fittings as well as unsold stock that I had to do something with. Putting them into storage was too expensive so after a lot of thought I chose to rent a very, very small shop just off the main shopping centre, next to the multi-storey car park for three months. I hoped that the new location and the much smaller shop would help to shift the remaining stock over the forthcoming Christmas period. I was even slightly hopeful that this would be the boost that the shop needed and it would make a little money to pay off all my loans.

I threw myself into getting rid of rubbish, dismantling what felt like hundreds of shelves and cabinets and filling countless skips. Gradually it came together and I was finally able to move into the smaller shop. I was hopeful that I would get custom from the constant stream of people walking past to the car park.

Chapter 4

Wants and Needs

It is not until you hit financial difficulties that you truly understand the difference between a want and a need. I spiralled into difficulties on a step process, and as I reached each plateau I was convinced at that time that I could not exist on less than I was, until I had to. I had surely cut back on all my extravagances, but the truth is that as I look back now, I was massively naive on what I actually needed to survive.

I did at one point have a reasonable income and was able to pay my bills and afford some luxuries, but did I appreciate and value what I had? No not at all. I used to go out and blow in one Saturday shopping trip with my Mum what I currently live on now for a month. I bought, I thought wisely, going to the sales. Buying the bag to go with the shoes, the three for two deals, a half price outfit.

When I lost my home and had to move my belongings into storage, I found clothes with price tags still on. Bottles of shampoo and cleaning products still in the original carrier bag, stuffed at the back of cupboards. Books I hadn't read yet, DVD's I hadn't watched. Tons of stuff I had accumulated over the years that to be honest I had never really looked at, after the day I bought it. I mean seriously who needs twelve cans of WD40!

If I had been forewarned that my financial problems were to become serious rather than a minor blip, I would have been quicker to put into practice ways to conserve and spend wisely my meagre income, rather than struggling with each new problem from the back foot. Maybe then I would have been able to get in front of my financial decline rather than racing to play catch up. But being in denial is a comfortable place to reside until you get metaphorically evicted.

We are surrounded day and night with advertising on what we should have, and when we are thrown into a situation where this is no longer possible, we often start to mentally come from a place of lack which further distresses us, and leads to self-destructive behaviours. I mean who hasn't at some point rushed out to buy an extra lottery ticket, when you know you are going to struggle to pay the bills this month? Or booked a weekend break on the credit card knowing that you will default on the minimum payment when the monthly payment is due, just to cheer ourselves up?

When we can't pay what is due we mentally torture ourselves about what we can no longer afford, and then dig ourselves a bigger hole by not addressing the issue and ordering out for a Chinese takeaway to make ourselves feel better, and on it goes.

We constantly compare ourselves to others and measure our self worth on what we have, but if tomorrow I waved a magic wand and gave everyone the exact same possessions and money forever how would you feel?

Cheated? I just took away your proof that you are someone.

But does it really make you a better person to have more, or a lesser person to have less? No you are still the same person regardless of the outer wrappings. I don't look at a multi-millionaire any differently to a homeless guy living on the street, so why should I worry about anyone looking at me differently, just because this year I'm doing well or next year life is a bit of a struggle. I am just at a point in my life where I am learning valuable lessons on what it means to be me. Most people at some point in their lives go through financial hardship and just because it is your turn, endeavour to just accept it as a fluid moment and do the best you can with it. Eventually like the seasons of life it will evolve and pass, and you will be the richer for having experienced it.

The more you panic and hold on to that feeling of lack the longer it will persist in your life. Be aware of what you still have and be grateful for it. There is always someone worse off than you so notice them and share what you can whatever that may be. Often after visiting the food bank I would see a guy huddled in a shop doorway. Now I didn't have enough money at the time to buy food, but I appreciated how lucky I was that I had a roof over my head, and I was no longer living in my van. I had a free bag of donated food at home waiting for me and I was grateful. Grateful to the supermarkets and their caring shoppers who didn't know me or my story, who made an effort to make my life just that little bit easier. So even though it wasn't much in the big scheme of things I made sure that I gave the homeless guy the change in my pocket so he could get himself a meal too. I'd take a moment to acknowledge his presence and say Hi and give him a smile, all these things I could afford to share and they made his life and mine even for a moment less harsh. So often I have heard from homeless people that it was lovely that someone actually took the time to truly see them, and say Hi, and that costs nothing.

If we all took a little time to understand the difference between a need and a want, and were grateful for what we had. We could all share something with someone who needs something. Now whether that is a sandwich for a homeless guy or a few moments listening to someone who is feeling sad and living alone in a big house, it doesn't matter by sharing what we have we are all happier in the long run. It is time to stop allowing society to dictate how we should be by trying to convince us that all our wants are needs because they really aren't. I know I would be a lot happier being surrounded by people who genuinely want to ensure we all have our needs met, than by people who are more worried that their flat screen TV is not as big as their neighbour's one.

So the worst has happened and you are struggling financially what do you do?

Take stock of where you are right now. Who do you owe? What have you got that would help the situation. Above all be honest with yourself and other people about what you are facing. There is no shame in having financial problems so don't convince yourself there is. The sooner you get help to deal with things the quicker you will feel better.

First things first though you have to understand your needs.

There are only five needs if you strip it down to pure basics.

Shelter

Warmth

Food

Water

Connection

I know you are going to say there are many more needs you want to include but they will always be wants. They are not essential to life.

Shelter takes the form of your home, a place to stay or protection from the weather. Depending on your circumstances you need some form of this. All of the programs I have seen on TV surprise me how often people are willing to buy practically anything else and be evicted than take responsibility and address this crucial need. Do not put your head in the sand on this one. Whatever small amount of money you get must first be on securing a place to sleep. Take advantage of any help that is available in your area, contact the council, talk to family, ask friends or contact charities. Don't wait until the last second, get planning. If you are going to have to move out then down size your possessions. The first time I had to downsize I put my possessions into storage and it cost me a fortune when I couldn't within a few months resolve the situation. Always plan that it may take longer than you think, and then you won't have a nasty surprise. There is no point being precious over your furniture it is second-hand anyway and it would be more use to you as cash rather than costing you money to store. When you are back on your feet you can replace the furniture.

Warmth may not be as important in summer but is vitally important during the winter months. Think about reducing the thermostat a few degrees. Use a blanket and put an extra jumper on. Have a look in the charity shops for a hat, gloves and warm coat and wear them. If you are facing more severe financial hardship talk to your energy provider on their schemes for low incomes, it is also often of benefit to move to a property that includes all the bills in the monthly rent, as it is often cheaper. Stay warm by going out to heated places, the library, friends and family, volunteer at a centre, a walk round the shopping centre or staying at work a little longer all help to cut the bill. In the depths of winter ensure you have adequate ventilation but try and reduce the heat in any rooms you don't use. Keep the curtains closed to keep the heat in. Try going to bed a little earlier and invest in a hot water bottle or a low cost electric blanket.

Food can be a major worry but to get the best while under financial difficulties you may have to be open to new experiences. Think instead of what do I want to eat tonight, and replace it with what is available and what nutrition do I need? You may have some unusual combinations but at least you won't be hungry. Ask at your supermarkets when they reduce the prices on goods that are on their sell by date, so you know when to turn up. Aim for fruit and vegetables and get whatever you can. There are often quite a few vegetables due to be thrown away. You are looking for a wide range of colours to ensure you have a good level of nutrition. Meat is expensive but we generally eat far too much in one sitting anyway. If you cut it up into small pieces it goes much further. I often make six meals out of a packet of six sausages by cutting them up into pieces and adding more vegetables. You still get the taste to satisfy but eat a lot more vegetables and less meat. Prepare all your meals and freeze them straight away as soon as you get home, that way you can make full use of those discounted products, and not just throw them away a couple of days later. If you have a garden you could even look at growing your own food too.

If you are unable to buy basic food due to a lack of income, then in the most difficult of circumstances you can turn to foodbanks and soup kitchens. These provide a small amount of food for those suffering extreme hardship. They are run by dedicated people who provide invaluable help to those in need. In order to access these you should contact the citizens' advice bureau who will be able to give you the details in your area. Please only access these services if you are truly in need as they are reliant on charitable donations and are often oversubscribed.

Water is vital to health. Try and replace most of your drinks with water. It is much better for you health wise, and cheaper than all the cans of drinks. Take a shower rather than a bath, as it uses less water. Think about your water usage and make cuts where you can. Do you need to use the washing machine or the dishwasher that often? Can you collect rain water to wash the car or water the garden?

Connection is important, and you may not think so, but it will make things so much easier for you and open you up to new opportunities. Just because you are having financial difficulties doesn't mean you become a hermit, in fact you should do the exact opposite within reason.

Don't be afraid to be honest about your situation. Confront the elephant in the room so to speak, it will make it much easier for you and others to deal with. They will keep an ear out for new ideas, and be able to make suggestions on things you had not thought of. Be open to making new friends too, for less expensive activities. Just because your old friends are going on an around the world cruise be happy for them, it doesn't mean you can't go on a picnic with them when they get back. Give up trying to compete, true friends don't care how much money you have. Pick and choose what activities are in your budget, and don't feel obligated to attend something you know you can't easily afford. Remember this is a temporary situation, so don't make it harder for yourself by digging a deeper debt hole, just because you couldn't say no now.

Chapter 5

Twenty Tips to Cut Costs

• To maintain your important need for connection it is often a great idea to go out with friends for a meal, but this will present its own difficulties when you are short of cash. Just remember this important point, no one will remember what you had, only that you were there, so order a starter for main course or use a children's meal. It is about the conversation not the food.

• Be proactive when you arrive and don't be scared, talk to the waitress in advance and get your own bill, that way you don't get caught at the end paying for your friend's numerous drinks and extras, even when you have been frugal on what you have ordered. Never split the bill at the end, you will always end up spending more than you intended to.

• If you are ordering a meal then to reduce the cost drink tap water for free, or ask for extra hot water if you are ordering a pot of tea. Most restaurants won't mind as long as you are paying for the food. This however probably won't work in a pub.

• In a pub remember that sharing time with your friends is far more important than drinking copious amounts of alcohol that you can't afford. Buy one if you really have to and make it last, but also look at drinking a squash which will be a fraction of the price or alternating with a cheaper soft drink.

• Once you are in financial difficulties be honest with yourself on the likely chances of you getting back in the black in the next month. If you are looking at years then there is no point in continuing to run up further debts you will only be making things worse for yourself. Cancel the credit cards, and don't take out pay day loans or further credit.

• If you can walk to where you need to be then leave the car at home where you can. It will save you money on the petrol, be good for the environment and it will make you fitter as a bonus.

• Empty those cupboards and use all those hoarded products that you have accumulated over the years. You may not like the smell of lavender but being clean is more important than buying your favourite shower gel when you have a lavender one in the cupboard.

• Soap is cheaper than the multitude of hand cleaners and shower gels that we adorn our bathrooms with. Look at the cheaper value brands because they can often be just as good just in cheaper packaging.

• Use cash. Aim to take out your money once a week. See how little you can get away with having. Having unlimited and invisible amounts of money on plastic, mean that it is very easy to lose track of what you are spending your money on and how much you have left. By seeing those last few coins in your purse or wallet it makes decisions on what you should or should not buy, much harder hitting and will reduce your spending.

• Get in contact with the people you owe money to as soon as you hit problems, and work with them to resolve the situation. They are often much more helpful if they don't have to track you down because you are hiding from them. On the opposite side of the equation if anyone owes you money now is the time to be brave and get them to set up a payment plan with you to repay the debt.

• Talk to Step Change they are the leading debt advice service in the UK and will help you to arrange repayment plans and give you advice on the best course of action for your particular circumstances, and level of debt. There are similar services available in other countries also. Be wary of those companies offering IVA's that will be taking a percentage of everything you pay to your creditors. You can sort out plans where all the money you pay off goes to your creditors.

- If you are entitled to benefits ensure you seek advice so that you have claimed everything that you are due.

- Stop spending money on things that you don't need. Recreational drugs, alcohol, cigarettes, gambling, junk food, beauty products, gadgets, etc. We all know they are fun but you do not need these things in your life and you will be much better off without them.

- Link up with other people and look at sharing or using a barter system for services. For example I'll babysit for you if you cut my hair. There are whole communities that work very effectively using this system and everyone benefits.

- Get some books from the library to learn new skills, and start recycling your own worn out products into something else. This can be very useful for times when presents are required.

- When it is your turn to receive presents for birthday or Christmas ask for what you need. You don't need a new ornament but you could do with a few bottles of your favourite shower gel or a gift voucher for the local supermarket so you have food in January.

- Have a look on places like Freecycle, for unwanted things that you could make use of. Keep an ear out with friends who want to get rid of stuff and haven't got the time. Offer to help, you might find something of use.

- Be honest with friends about your situation, you won't be the only one. Invite friends to yours rather than go out for coffee. You can have just as much fun with a DVD and they will probably bring a bottle of wine to share.

- Look at constructing a budget so you can easily see where you can make savings and record your payments. Ensure you are getting the best most competitive packages for your money, and don't be afraid to switch. You can even use a diary to record all of your cash expenses over the week. It can be a real eye opener when you see how much you have spent on things you could have done without.

• If you have an extra room then take advantage of the government's rent a room scheme and make yours pay. It also might be time to have that difficult conversation with those who live with you about paying their way in the household. Young adults especially can assume that even though their parents are struggling to make ends meet that it doesn't apply to them. Agree a budget and don't be afraid to ask for a contribution you are not doing them any favours in their future homes by not teaching them how to budget now. Being there for kids by talking and listening is often much more useful than throwing money at them.

Chapter 6

A New Start?

The sun for once was shining brightly as I opened the door of the new shop. It was much smaller than the other shop being about a tenth of the size. It consisted of freshly painted white walls with a toilet and sink out the back. It had none of the character of the old shop but I was hoping for a newer image. It was a little bit of a challenge trying to find a way to fit what was left from the old shop within its walls, but we did eventually manage to accomplish it.

I had agreed to take on the lease for a period of only three months, having learnt from my previous experience that it would be better to get a feel for the area, before signing up for a longer term. I was confident that I would be making that commitment.

The new shop was a few miles away from the old one in Southend on a bustling street that connected one of the main multi-storey car parks with the high street, and although it didn't get quite as much foot traffic as the high street, it came a good second. With Christmas quickly approaching it seemed like the ideal place for my fortunes to change.

I had been left with one Saturday member of staff after the recent move, and my daughter was keen to give me a hand for a few hours, so we made the shop look as inviting as we could, and did our best to encourage some new custom.

During those first few weeks there I chose to concentrate on the positives of my situation and began making some new plans. I did quickly realise though that I should have kept a closer eye on my young staff while I was doing it.

One Saturday I was busily working away adding up figures when I became aware that the shop was becoming unusually busy. I was obviously quite pleased but also a little confused, as a number of people were peering in through the window, walking in and then walking out again without buying anything. Intrigued to find out what was attracting their attention and getting them through the door, I stepped outside to be confronted by a large sign with the letters BOOBS emblazoned prominently across the window.

Shocked I brought the sign to the attention of my sniggering staff who very innocently said I should take a closer look. Peering much closer I noticed some very small lettering between each capital which when read together produced the words Big Offers On Binoculars Sale. I had to laugh.

If I had been selling boobs rather than cameras I would have made a fortune.

Behind the scenes though, I was still covering up a multitude of problems that I just couldn't face dealing with. My relationship was going from bad to worse and I was starting to feel that I wasn't even in one anymore. I felt cheap and used. I couldn't depend on my boyfriend being there when he said he would. Customers were turning up to see him, the boss, even though I was the owner of the shop, and he wouldn't be there, and he was the only one they wanted to talk to. Promises he made to them weren't being kept, which didn't help the reputation of the shop. Eventually I had to tell him that if he wasn't going to follow through with his promises then he shouldn't make them. So he stopped and lost interest.

Shortly afterwards I received notification that the car park providing the shaky life line for my business was to close and be taken down sometime in the following year.

The council quickly cordoned off the end of the road and prevented through access. Overnight my few customers vanished. The road became a cul-de-sac of no-one. It was a dead end road with my shop at the end. My temporary rental ended in the middle of January and my dreams of having a successful Christmas period were rudely destroyed.

I felt totally overwhelmed with the amount of issues I was dealing with.

Chapter 7

Where am I? Fighting the Overwhelm

If you are anything like me you don't just have one issue you have multiple issues and they have their own issues all breeding like rabbits. When I was going through one of my darkest periods I was dealing with a number of issues some very obvious, and some not so obvious to me. I therefore totally understand the huge amounts of mindless negative chatter swirling around in your head and the dark cloud enveloping and suffocating what little air you have left. Nothing makes you smile. Tears are just moments away, and you are so tired that you feel you could sleep for a week, but every time you try your eyes remain firmly open glued to the clock as it registers 3am. You spend hours staring at the cracks in the wall or tracing the pattern of the wallpaper with your finger, and the pressure of time weighs heavily on you. There is so much to do and not enough time, but again hours slip by on pointless activities achieving nothing. You resort to jumping from one disaster to another desperately fire-fighting and patching up. People around you don't understand and you can't face communicating anymore so you withdraw into yourself and hide away. Sound familiar?

We have all done it at some point in our lives. This I call "Overwhelm" and it creeps up on you without warning. It wants to bury you alive with problems and emotions until you can't see a way out. It makes you so tired that you feel like a zombie. It isolates you from peer support and destroys your self-worth. It wants to whisper in your ear, lies and half truths and saps your will-power to zero. One of its greatest enemies though is "Recognition".

Recognition takes the sting out of Overwhelm even by just at your worst moment saying to yourself out loud, "I'm in Overwhelm" is enough to make your mind pause and go "ooh that's interesting?". Recognition makes your mind take a mental note of where it is and helps it to list the issues, so it can find the one that is buried at the bottom of the pile and causing the most problem. I found it helped me enormously.

So let's give "Recognition" a bit of an airing and see what it has to contribute for you.

We first have to be honest with ourselves about what we are facing. It is time to stop running away and just quietly sit with what is affecting us.

If you have debt problems then opening the letters instead of hiding them in the bread bin would be an example. In an abusive situation it would be accepting that you either have been or are being abused. With a romantic relationship it could be that you need to accept it is over or that there are problems. With a health condition it is acknowledging that your health problem will impact on your life. Depression is very much a condition I think where you just suddenly lose the ability to communicate. So to help you to ease the pain before it becomes critical, grab yourself a piece of paper and see if you can write down one sentence describing what each issue is, and leave a space underneath.

My partner has walked out on me.

My business has collapsed

My health is bad

My boyfriend is hitting me

I have no friends

My credit card is maxed out

Now with your list look at the biggest obstacle to your leaving this situation behind starting with the word "I".

My partner has walked out on me.

I love him and I can't imagine life without him

My business has collapsed

I feel a failure and my family will suffer

My health is bad

I won't be able to live my life the way I want to.

My boyfriend is hitting me

I won't be able to cope on my own

I have no friends

I don't like who I am so why will anyone else

My credit card is maxed out

I think my family is going to starve

Read the new sentences to yourself and spend a moment noticing where in your body you feel the sensations. Are you feeling them in your heart or chest? Maybe it is a weight on your shoulders or emptiness in the pit of your stomach? Is there pain in your back or heartburn?

The mind has a profound effect on the body and you will often find that emotional problems manifest and worsen physical issues within the body, if you don't take action to resolve them.

Take your sentences and now re-write them positively even if you currently don't believe them.

My partner has walked out on me.

I love him and I can't imagine life without him

I love myself and I can imagine a wonderful life

My business has collapsed

I feel a failure and my family will suffer

I am a success and my family will prosper

My health is bad

I won't be able to live my life the way I want to.

I will be able to live a full productive life.

My boyfriend is hitting me

I won't be able to cope on my own

I can cope on my own

I have no friends

I don't like who I am so why will anyone else

I like who I am and so do other people.

My credit card is maxed out

I think my family is going to starve

I know my family has plenty of food

Saying these new positive sentences to yourself out loud will hinder any overwhelm and focus your mind elsewhere, giving you that much needed break from constantly being bombarded by cruel unrelenting negative thoughts. The new statements may make you squirm a bit but with practice the positive statements will become easier to say.

You will also start to notice that lurking underneath almost hidden is fear. This is your fear of change. Surprised? I was too when I first noticed that pretty much all the long term insurmountable problems I had ever had were made worse by one thing a fear of change.

So how can saying a few positive phrases help you ask. Well I find the mind requires around ten positive phrases per negative one before it breaks the pattern and starts to let go, and allows us to notice positive resolutions to our problems.

Now you can choose to put down this book and I sincerely hope you don't, and continue to be re-active to your current situation. Cementing it into being with negative thought, after negative thought, or you can choose to face the fear and give things a try. Being pro-active in your journey is the key. I am not saying it will be easy but I am going to say it will be worth it. Accept the fact that in order to improve things then you will have to do something to change, and you are going to have to be ok with that however scary that may be.

Write out all of your positive phrases and tape them to your mirror. Every morning and night read out loud to yourself each phrase ten times. If you have more than five phrases then pick the top five that are affecting you. Continue this until you can easily do it without feeling silly or awkward. Do it until you can say them with a genuine smile and a feeling of peace.

During the day if you catch yourself internally hearing the negative phrases, just loudly say "Stop" and if you can remember, replace the negative phrase with your positive one.

We all know someone whether a celebrity or someone close to you who has gone through a tough time and they still manage to smile, they still care about other people's problems. They are the first to offer a listening ear. They go out of their way to make a difference both big and small no matter what hand life has dealt them. These people have harnessed their negative mind chatter, instinctively and are actively changing it to positive. On the other side of the coin there are many people who have experienced the same devastating circumstances, who withdraw from the world and are unable to cope with life. Spiralling down into depression, until tragically they can no longer cope, these are the ones whose negative mind chatter reproduces unchecked.

It is not dictated who naturally gets to be on one side of the coin or the other by vast amounts of money, being super successful, being loved by everyone or even they are just plain lucky. Often genetics and life experience can bring you more firmly on one side than the other to start with, but in reality the only difference is their **current** state of mind. It doesn't matter whether you are a super star, or a homeless guy, or which side of the coin their genetics started them, both can influence their state of mind if they know how to, and they want to, for FREE.

Chapter 8

The Discard

I trusted my boyfriend completely and I believed deeply in him. I wouldn't have thought twice about running into a burning building to save him such was my faith. I put him on a pedestal and practically worshipped at his feet. I never questioned anything I believed that we were soul mates. Our relationship wasn't conventional by any means but I thought that we had a deep unbreakable connection that went beyond a romantic relationship. I had known him for many years before we dated as a friend. However, with hindsight I now realise how often I made excuses to cover up the inconsistencies. How I lied to myself in order to keep the illusion going.

It was November a few days before my daughter's birthday and strangely for once both my boyfriend and I had been in the shop. Business was not good and he had been off and distracted all day. I sort of knew what was coming so I just asked him as he dropped me off at home. Did he have another girl and he admitted that yes he did have an interest in another girl but absolutely nothing had happened.

Surprisingly he cried and I sat there in shock while he apologised and said that we would be better as friends and I agreed. I said it was ok and walked into my room. I was numb and sad that we would not be having a romantic relationship but I understood that I wasn't good enough and I was relieved that the most important part of our relationship to me would remain intact. He would still be there for me. I just couldn't face life without referring to my man on the pedestal. I posted on Facebook about our amicable decision to part and wished him well.

I knew it would be difficult to adjust but if I could keep my soul mate as my best friend, then it would be worth it.

Chapter 9

Who is in My Corner?

I went through many years in my personal journey looking to the wrong people for help, before I figured out that the answer to this particular question makes things a whole lot easier to deal with. I wish I had worked it out at the beginning but maybe life was keen to help me understand the draw backs of not putting this in practice first. So in order to make your journey a little less difficult I am putting it here at the beginning where it should be.

In all good therapy everyone talks about the inner circle, and who should be in it, but I am going to take it one step further and say that there should be no-one in your inner circle other than positive you, and the reason I say that is that no matter how wonderful a friend or relative is, they are going to have an off day occasionally, because they are human.

I have lost count of the times where I have been supporting someone going through a tough time, and they have been floored by a throw away comment made by their nearest and dearest who is just plain having a bad day.

So inside this inner circle is only you, your positive self, or if you like your higher self if you are spiritual. She or He loves you unconditionally no matter what. The love for you is so huge that you can't even imagine it. They will always cheer you on when you struggle. They are the ones saying your positive statements in the mirror to you. Close your eyes and imagine for a moment standing on cool green grass inside a large circle. Open your arms wide and feel golden energy wrapping itself lovingly around you. This is your own unconditional love and you can tap into this anytime you want or need to and you should.

My rule now is that no-one is allowed to breach this inner circle boundary, that way I can always view life's challenges from a place of stability rather than be constantly at the mercy of other people's tidal waves of emotional torment.

The event has happened, however where you view it from makes a difference to how you cope with it.

Outside your inner circle is another circle. This circle is for people who make you feel good and are supportive. Now you are probably thinking that family should be in here by default but no, they shouldn't. To start with put everyone you know on the outside of the outer circle. This may seem a little extreme but it gives you a chance to evaluate each individual relationship and see if it is supportive or not. If they are your best friend, or your husband, they shouldn't be allowed to sneak past your evaluation system into your circle without being tested. Look carefully do they talk about you nicely, are they there for you when you need them. Do you feel loved and appreciated in their company or do you feel on edge and constantly apologising? Do these people take advantage of you emotionally, financially or physically? Don't worry though, over time people will naturally flow in and out of your circle and that is ok, but it is good to know who is where so you can allocate your time accordingly.

People who remain on the outside of the circles, and that **includes negative you**, are still important, but you know that there are issues or difficulties in these relationships, and you have to be more aware of the dynamics when you are dealing with these individuals, and ensure you protect yourself from harm.

You are probably now panicking that your supportive people list is either zero or not very big. Relax that is normal. In the middle of a crisis we often only see those people in our lives that are right in our face, and who sometimes shouldn't even be in our circle at all. By doing this exercise it will give you an opportunity to see the wood from the trees.

It is a bit like having a good clear out at home. Going through the loft and the garage and piling up all the stuff you have accumulated over the years that you trip over every day or squeeze past, and finally getting it out of your space. Having that space then allows you to have a shop around, and choose what you really want to put in it, and not what you inherited from Great Aunt Mary.

We all have a finite amount of time in this life, and it is better for you if you spend more of your precious time with people that are good for you than bad. I don't suggest you suddenly dump everyone bad but gradually be aware of how much time they take up and how little joy you get from the interaction. By spending less time with them they will make an unconscious choice to either adjust their behaviour to match your increased self worth or to accept their new place outside your circles.

You will find that some of the people who you previously had no time for, and you barely knew, have taken a step into your supportive circle just because they treat you well. Maybe with a little more time you could be surprised at how close you could be.

Have a look at organisations and clubs that would interest or support you as they can be a valuable resource of supportive people, anything from the obvious AA meetings, to Gingerbread, and food banks could be useful, depending on your circumstances. There are also singles nights, adult education and bereavement groups. The list goes on and on. The thing to remember is that you are not alone, there are many people in the world who are, have or will struggle just as you are, and they are all waiting for you to take the first step and reach out and connect. I found a great comfort in talking to similarly depressed people in the US online anonymously during my sleepless nights while I waited for my life to sort itself out.

To clarify the term I loosely use supportive people to mean those who treat you well and that doesn't have to be people you pour your heart out to for hours. They can just be people who take your mind off your problems, make you smile or offer a helping hand. The work mate who saves you a seat at the meeting, the lady in the cafe who remembers how you like your tea or even the guy who helps you on to the bus with your heavy bags. Sometimes during my worst moments, I have had a glimpse of happiness just by a silly joke from a stranger. Don't under estimate their value of diminishing the darkness while your best mate is busy. Just make sure you include them in your circle.

What you are trying to achieve here is a way to open your life up to more than it just being about your problem. We, when under stress, often keep focusing in on the problem and then focus even more until our whole life is twenty-four seven just the problem, and we can't see a way out. By spending time with our supportive people even if it is only the lady in the cafe or the guy on the bus and being in the moment and conscious of what is happening, we remove the extreme focus on the problem and replace it with some happier moments which we can then build on. We need to be grateful for every single one of them as they are the key to engaging our brain on positive thoughts. When our brains are relaxed then change becomes easier to cope with and solutions appear with ease.

The other good thing that this exercise will do for you is free up some time for you to use for yourself.

Chapter 10

The Aftermath

There was a party a couple of days after we split up that I had been invited to with a mutual group of friends and I knew he would be there. I missed talking to him and wanted to catch up. So I thought I would make an effort and go along. The minute I walked in you could have cut the atmosphere with a knife. If my friends could have pushed me back out of the door they probably would have. No-one could look me in the eye and then I found out why, he'd brought his new serious girlfriend who he had been at a wedding with weeks before.

Everyone already knew all about her and she was now a firm fixture in the group. I was incredibly hurt that no-one had told me and felt he could have taken her somewhere else and at least given me a little time. We had after all been dating on and off for seven years so I didn't think it would have been out of the realms of possibility for him to give me a couple of months to adjust before I was usurped by my replacement. I was annoyed that he was continually commenting on how much younger she was and playing her off against the other new girlfriends in the group. I bit my lip and was polite although I doubt neither she nor me were very comfortable. I felt ousted by everyone as they were all doing their best to avoid having to get involved. I understand now but at the time it only made matters worse and I felt like everyone thought I was over reacting or totally insane, especially since he had been implying behind my back, that we weren't really together at all.

He loudly promised to text me and we parted ways.

Chapter 11

Understanding the Warning Signs

We are all surrounded by people who aren't good for us, so here are some of the red flags you should be on the look-out for, when trying to identify toxic people within your circle. Not every toxic person will exhibit every one of these, but if they have more than a couple you should be on your guard.

Toxic people will do their best to blend in but the most obvious is that you feel on-edge around this person and you are not sure why. They set themselves slightly above you which either makes you look up to them in some way or puts you in a competitive position.

You feel you have to prove yourself and find yourself actively competing for their attention.

You become the butt of every joke and put down they can throw your way.

If they deem to give you their attention you often feel like the sun is shining down on you and you have achieved celebrity status.

As these relationships develop subtle changes will start to appear.

You do your best not to rock the boat and will "walk on eggshells" as at any moment they could fly into a rage or leave you. You will literally find the most awkward way to do something rather than risk upsetting them.

They will restrict your other family or friendship relationships, through either direct aggressive control tactics, such as stopping you from seeing them physically or making such a drama you can't face going. They can also use covert abandonment tactics by excluding you from events directly or as a consequence of their actions.

They lie, withhold affection or give the silent treatment rather than discuss their problems rationally, they also never admit fault of any sort and imply everything is your problem.

They cheat, triangulate with previous partners and blatantly or covertly erode your self esteem by putting you down with snide or jokey comments, or by implying you are needy after ignoring you for three days. They are also fond of the 1am booty call or the vanishing act the morning after.

They will become overly involved in commenting about your personal appearance, what and how you wear things, and will pick up and relay every real and perceived fault both to your face and behind your back.

They have no personal boundaries and will quite happily use up whatever resources you have while vehemently protecting their own from you. Sharing only works one way with these people and once your drained they will move on.

They will be only too happy to share with you what everyone thinks about you and will often be at the bottom of any unfounded rumours circulating.

After ending a relationship with a toxic person you will feel insane, exhausted, drained, shocked, suicidal, and empty.

What you have to understand with toxic people, is that they will use your worst insecurities against you, so by ensuring that your own inner voice is on your side always and giving you positive reinforcement, you can quickly identify and protect yourself from having closer relationships with these sorts of people.

For example if I called you a pink giraffe with blue spots would you have an emotional response to it? Probably not as at no time have you ever called yourself that, so you would shrug it off and not accept it into your psyche.

However, if I called you ugly you would have an emotional response to that, as at one time or another we have all thought of ourselves that way. There is no difference it is just words in each case but the impact is what you choose to believe in yourself. So if you're inner voice is saying you are ugly, then how much easier is it for a toxic person to get a foothold in your life by using exactly the same term. They are masters at finding the words we use against ourselves.

So instead when someone calls you a name don't accept it. It is their issue, and you have no evidence to support that conclusion because you don't view yourself that way, and as it is a comment designed to upset and undermine you that person is immediately removed from your outer circle, and unless they do significant work on themselves should never be allowed back inside your outer circle again.

Identifying and restricting the damage toxic people can do in your life as quickly as possible prevents long term damage. Yes it would be nice not to have toxic people messing up your life, and for the extreme examples no contact is probably the way to go, but they do exist in everyday life and finding a way to manage relationships with the ones you have to have contact with sometimes becomes a necessity.

It goes without saying though that if someone is abusive towards you physically, even if they apologise and promise it will never happen again, they don't get a second chance ever and should be immediately reported to the police and full action should be taken to protect yourself and your family. No matter how much these people beg and plead if they have physically hurt you once they will do it again, and it may not be today or tomorrow but it will be one day, and do you really want to live "walking on eggshells" until that happens. Too many people have been seriously injured or died doing that. It may only be a shove or a slap now, but next time it could be a fist or a knife. Don't wait. Get out at the first hint, your worth more than that.

The one thing I want to remind you is that checking whether someone is good for us should be a task you do on a regular basis. If someone's behaviour has suddenly changed towards us then it is time to have another little check and take action if necessary.

Chapter 12

What the F*!**

Over the next few weeks we played a sick game where my Ex would promise and then fail to deliver on our friendship. It was one of the cruellest ways to destroy someone. You should either be in a friendship or not, you can't only be in one when other people are watching.

Excuse followed excuse, half truth after lie, constantly being shown how he could be very romantic and caring with his new girlfriend, things he swore he could never do with me. Buying gifts, making her feel special, holidays away, meeting his family for Sunday dinner, which I never got to do and his plans to get a flat together.

I'd accepted long ago that he wasn't that sort of guy and that was fine, but then to be confronted with the fact that he was capable of doing all those things, but it was just he didn't value me enough to ever want to do them with me, even before I'd hit financial difficulties and lost my house.

I was and always had been nothing to him but a convenient sexual stop gap in between his many flings until someone better came along, and that realisation really hurt.

My mind began an internal argument that neither side could win. The rare times I saw him he was overly attentive in public with grandiose friendship promises and I'd catch glimpses of the man I knew and feel yes he did want to remain friends but this was followed by an astounding inability to reply to a text message, or remember any of those promises. I'd wait days for an answer and then I'd bump into him and he would be pleased to see me and feign surprise at what he had agreed. Apologise and promise again only for him to supposedly forget yet again.

We would play the game again and again. I felt like I was going crazy, where was the guy who was supposed to be my friend, maybe it was me, was I overstepping boundaries? No I had made it clear the romantic relationship was over permanently. I treated his girl-friend with respect and was keen to ensure that she was fully informed about our friendship and made an effort to become friends with her so what was going on? I felt like I was being forced into playing the stalker ex-girlfriend. No-one else wanted to get involved or could see what was happening. I was making excuse after excuse for him until eventually I ran out of excuses. How could a man that I respected and loved unconditionally that I had bent over backwards to accommodate with his new girlfriend treat me like that? It was at this point that I shattered completely. I couldn't reconcile the man I believed to be my soul-mate the one who was forever telling our friends what close friends we were, with the one who was treating me so badly by completely ignoring me the rest of the time. My mind imploded and shut down. I'd lost my soul-mate in fact he had never really existed at all, he was just a figment of my own twisted imagination. Nothing would ever be the same again.

Life just stopped for me. The pain was something I can't even describe. I can't just say I cried because it was more than that, I cried from my soul. I had absolutely nothing left to live for anymore.

I'd lost my soul mate, my boyfriend, my best mate, my kids, my home, my friends, my business was in ruins, and I was massively in debt. I truly believed that I would not survive.

Day after day I lay in bed and cried for hours till I fell asleep, only to wake crying a few hours later. It was a grief that never seemed to end, and never eased. I didn't care anymore. I just wanted the pain to stop. I stopped eating, couldn't sleep and spent hours upon hours staring blankly at the wall. Tortured by the relentless negative self talk twenty-four seven. My hair fell out and I developed a bizarre skin condition that appeared over night.

Patches of skin just scabbed over, blistered and bled. I was deeply tired and suffered from panic attacks, palpitations, indigestion and constipation. I was a complete mess.

Chapter 13

Mind Over Matter

We have all had to deal with a broken heart where a relationship has just not worked out, but we knew who that person was. We can understand the relationship from their point of view. We acknowledge and work through together the separation process. We gradually separate our lives and we make an effort to be considerate of our ex-partners feelings. It may not always work out that way but we make an effort.

We go through a period of grief at the loss and we miss them. We say goodbye to all the future plans we had for the relationship and we spend time with friends before reaching out and engaging in the social scene and meeting new people and new potential partners. We look at the good parts of the relationship and acknowledge honestly the less than perfect parts. It is a natural part of the relationship process and is painful but ultimately a necessary part of finding what works for us and is relatively short lived.

The aftermath of a toxic encounter is nothing like that, because the victim can suffer from cognitive dissonance. The definition that Wikipedia gives for the term cognitive dissonance is that it is the mental stress or discomfort experienced by an individual that holds two or more contradictory beliefs at the same time. It is an internal argument of the mind that neither side can win.

Cognitive dissonance isn't short lived it can go on for many years and is highly destructive unless suitable action is taken. It hides in plain sight under a relationship breakup for a person who has a more empathic persona from someone who has sociopathic tendencies. At its very worst it can be deadly causing the victim to withdraw from all support, suffer mental torment and self destructive activities including suicide.

The most important thing to get your head around is that the internal argument in your head about how could the person you knew actually be this person, or that person, is that it doesn't have to be either or it can just for now be both. For you at this moment in time just accept that.

It will stop the constant internal argument and allow you a moment of peace to gather your thoughts and to learn how to focus them elsewhere.

I have for quite a while had an interest in meditation and more recently in its latest form mindfulness. I personally think that skill has been very helpful to me over the years and right now for you it is important to learn at least a basic level, so that your thoughts come under your own control again and you are able to at least some of the time relax.

Speaking to a lot of people they are under the impression that it is very difficult to do and will take up vast amounts of time, but if you just clear ten minutes a day you will rapidly notice a calmer happier you emerging and it is no harder than closing your eyes and talking in your head to yourself in a good way. I much prefer to use the guided meditation where the narrator describes a scenario and you imagine it in your mind, but that is just my preference. If you feel more comfortable emptying your mind of all the clutter and letting go of all thoughts then go with that instead. If you struggle with visualisation then maybe your best way to learn isn't visually therefore try to do it kinaesthetically, in other words by feeling instead of seeing the pictures.

Try this exercise if pictures in your mind are difficult. Close your eyes and concentrate on feeling yourself breathing in and out nice and slowly, when you are comfortable doing that. Take your attention to your toes. Scrunch up your toes then relax them in each foot in turn. Then focus on your calf muscles and contract each one then relax. Do the same with your thigh muscles and gradually work your way up your body until you reach your scalp. Remember to breathe as you do this. It should take about ten minutes to complete and you will feel relaxed and calm.

I think that the mind is like a muscle when it is in tip top condition and regularly trained through meditation it becomes strong enough to focus on whatever you want it to. I have personally been able to use meditation in a number of ways the most recent being during my two years of bad health. I was able to successfully reduce my panic, heart rate and breathing to go through a number of unpleasant medical testing procedures so that they were much less stressful than anticipated.

If you are trying to use meditation to improve your health or focus while you are going through your difficulties ensure that you make a picture in your mind of what you want to see. For example don't see an image of your bad knee getting better instead see yourself walking across the fields with joy in your heart. Feel how strong and healthy you are.

When the mind isn't trained then it hasn't the strength to maintain its focus on what you choose but becomes tired and slips into allowing whatever unproductive thought is floating by to slip through so by having an image of your bad knee getting better a slip in focus will end up as just a bad knee.

There have been some interesting preliminary studies where athletes who regularly meditate and visualise a particular action, will perform better even if they don't physically practice the action they are visualising than those athletes who don't visualise at all. The muscles respond to the mental stimulation as much as the physical repetition.

I firmly believe that if you focus and believe enough you can manifest whatever you want or on the other side whatever you don't want. It is a two edged sword and if you focus on negative things as I said before such as I'm not good enough to do that, or I don't deserve to have nice things happen then they will outweigh the positive.

With regular meditation training you can ensure that you spend more time manifesting helpful things in your life rather than unhelpful and I know now which I would prefer.

Chapter 14

Happy New Year

New Year's Eve loomed ahead and I had had enough at that time I didn't want to be in pain anymore I just wanted it to stop. I had no concept of anyone caring about me. I felt totally alone betrayed and abandoned by the world. Only someone who has come that close to ending it will understand the depths of despair that I was experiencing.

You can't describe it other than to say it is a bottomless black hole of excruciating pain that literally takes your breath away. There is no light. There is no hope just a desire so strong not to be in pain again. During that time I am ashamed to admit that I didn't think of what the consequences of my actions would be to those I left behind. So if you are facing your own bottomless pit right now then I urge you to see those around you. Right now you may totally believe that no-one cares about you, that the world would be a better place without you, but you are very wrong.

Someone somewhere cares about you.

 I do.

Depression is a devastating illness and its symptoms make us believe that we are alone but in reality we are not. Trust me when I say that even though you may be having the worst time ever it will eventually end and better times will appear. But for divine intervention I wouldn't be here writing this to you right now. One day you too could be telling someone your story of survival in the darkest times, and if that is the only thing that keeps you fighting then use it. Don't miss out on that opportunity to change someone's life to make a difference. How many others who were successful in their attempts didn't get the chance to see how deeply they affected those around them? Didn't get a chance to realise that the bottomless pit they were in was just a dip in the long up and down road of life. Whatever you are facing things change, and you can find peace I promise you without throwing your life away.

I had been invited to a New Year's Eve Party at my ex-husband's and although I had said I would go I had no intention of going.

I didn't really plan it I just sort of ended up driving towards the town centre. I couldn't stop the tears from falling. I'd briefly stopped at the local hospital and walked into A & E but they were so busy that I didn't want to waste anyone's time so I'd walked out again. I couldn't communicate how I felt there were no words. I just wanted someone anyone to know how much pain I was in and to stop it. A pain so intense that I was struck dumb I literally couldn't say how I felt. How desperate and how totally lost I was. So I'd driven to town clutching a pair of pants the only thing that my ex-boyfriend had left behind (clean I might add) and sat in the van with a pen and a piece of paper. Why couldn't it have been a jacket or a shirt that would have been less cringe-worthy but no it was a pair black pants. I knew I was meant to write a last note, but I had nothing to say. I couldn't even write how I felt it was that horrific so I didn't. I just walked down the road towards the shop and the closed car park.

The bitter wind whipped around my neck and my breath hung in the frigid air. The ends of my fingers tingled with the cold as I shoved them deeper into my worn jacket pockets. Time became very slow as suddenly I contemplated the trajectory I would have to achieve in order to jump from the top storey of the car park and land in front of the shop. I imagined my broken body lying in front of the shop in full gothic gore my blood seeping into the rubbish-strewn gutter. The flashing police lights on the hastily erected cordon as they turned curious New Year's Eve revellers from the gruesome sight. The newspaper article and front page picture detailing my demise. I was totally focused on the end result and aching for release from the hell I was in.

I rounded the corner and entered the road where my shop was but instead of the car park, I was met with half a car park, the workmen had started early and demolished the bit I wanted to jump from and placed enhanced security around the rest to stop anyone getting close.

I was stunned and then the thing that probably saved my life happened. I finally got angry, very angry. I screamed, swore and cried.

"How dare you do that!"

"Hadn't I taken enough already and now I couldn't even jump off the bloody car park".

My anger now released grew and grew and grew. Repressed for so long it took on a life of its own and I was angry with the shop, the universe, everyone in the world and finally my now ex boyfriend and I was so angry. The anger burned in my veins heating my freezing body.

I suddenly couldn't control myself I marched down to the middle of the High Street which was full of party goers and pinned his pants to a park bench in the middle of the high street and carefully wrote down his mobile number on the piece of paper with a message that anyone who read it should give him a call on my behalf. With hindsight it probably wasn't the most mature thing to do, and it did piss him off a lot I heard later, but the anger and the thought of the calls he would receive made the pain just a little easier to deal with. So although I am sorry now for my childish behaviour I don't regret it one bit. Without that fluke I wouldn't be here now.

Exhausted I got back in the car and drove to the New Year's Eve Party as required and quietly sat in the kitchen with a cup of tea, watching as the world carried on around me.

Chapter 15

How to Recover from a Toxic Encounter

This whole exercise is about rescuing the part of you that you have lost, and at no point is it about reconciling with the person who has caused this situation.

When recovering from a toxic encounter that has caused cognitive dissonance, in other words conflicting internal view points, it is important to accept that both the bad traits and the good traits are true for you at this moment in time, it is important that you name the bad traits with your toxic person's real name. For this particular example I am going to use the term he although your toxic person could be of either gender. If you want to name your fantasy version then do but I found it easier not to.

During my healing process whenever I felt the loss of those manufactured traits I would talk to the good traits version. The perceived empathy, the interest in what I was doing, how I loved them and missed them. All the things I was denied doing by the real person's silent treatment. I was careful to ensure that this persona gradually looked less and less like him until in my mind's eye it was just a ball of pure white energy.

On the flip side as I became aware of the toxic person's less than supportive behaviour and the reality of how and what they thought of me. I would express myself to the bad traits persona. I would ensure I could see in my mind's eye an ethereal version of the real person.

Once you get to a point where every thought to do with them is allocated to the correct persona rather than the real person you can move on to the next stage.

Sit quietly with your eyes closed. Imagine yourself in a big silver bubble protected above and below, back and front, left and right. Bring in focus outside your bubble the bad traits persona. Really look at them floating in front of you with all of their issues. Look at them as though you are really seeing them for the first time. The way that they put you down, aren't there for you, make you think that it is your entire fault, the need to not be truthful about who they are. Now imagine talking to the persona and telling them that you deserve much better than what they are offering. See them nodding and agreeing.

Look down in your mind's eye at your body and see a number of long cords that connect from your body to their body. Take a great big pair of scissors and one by one sever each cord. Watch as you blast each end of the cords with white light from your finger and see the cords shrivel up and disappear. When you are done see him turn and walk away. Re-confirm that you are totally protected by your silver bubble and then open your eyes.

There will now probably be a gap of time. If any negative thoughts persist then say "Stop" if there is more than the odd negative one then re-do the exercise. Depending on the level of damage and the length of time it might be necessary to do it two to three times. Each time though you will feel a lightening of the negative load.

When you feel ready you can then deal with the good traits persona. For this one I found having a metaphorical funeral worked best. I visualised sitting on the beach talking to the white energy bubble. Hearing it talk to me about how it was all the parts of myself that I had lost track of during the relationship mirrored back to me. I then visualised it disappearing into the clouds above and being left with a sense of warmth and contentment knowing that I was once again whole.

During these mental exercises you will also need to take practical actions. The first is to remove this person outside your outer circle. Practice the word "No" and remember it doesn't matter what comes out of their mouth you are not allowing them to enter your circle or your inner world. That applies to them being nice and also nasty. Your self-worth comes from you now. You can get reassurance from those proven trustworthy in your circle if you need to but choose those people carefully. Often after a relationship, mutual friends will be recruited to the toxic person's way of thinking temporarily, don't panic just move them outside your circle. Give them time and they will make their own decisions and you can reallocate them if necessary at that time.

Your aim is that the toxic person can be in your vicinity and you don't want to declare your undying love for them or want to punch them on the nose. You should feel totally neutral.

Once you have achieved this state the toxic person may well try and engage you in playing one of their games to illicit an emotional response because they are going to notice that you aren't reacting anymore. Now you are aware that you are just playing a game for their amusement you can quickly and easily shut the game down and refuse to play.

For example a game of triangulation can be thwarted by complimenting the person they are trying to play you off against or refusing to look at your perceived rival and feigning boredom. Eventually they will get bored and lose interest in trying to provoke you.

You can then hold a functional interaction if you have to for the purposes of children or work, although, you will have to be on the lookout for any attempts to resurrect drama. Again don't play and be boring.

By learning these lessons and being aware of how toxic people behave you will not only be more aware of those toxic people you have already identified, but also not have to move to a remote island to avoid them. You will also be able to spot new toxic people who are trying to get into your life before they do any damage and be able to quickly remove them to outside your circle.

Chapter 16

Putting Myself First

I began to recognise that I had been constantly rushing from one relationship to another desperate to feel loved and worthy. I was terrified to actually face being totally on my own.

The thing about being alone is that it is during this time you actually get an insight into yourself and your own behaviour patterns. You can't hide or make excuses it just is what it is. I began to realise that my core belief system was one of "not good enough" and I unconsciously chose people to promote that belief system. My self-worth was totally gained from other people and not from myself. Every time I was let down or treated badly I would turn it inward on myself. I would make excuses for others behaviours, justify it and accept responsibility for not being attractive enough, thin enough, a good enough partner, not intelligent enough, a whole host of not good enough comments that I took to heart and mentally tortured myself with. I would look at their previous and current partners and wonder why they never treated them the same way. I became whatever they wanted me to be and I had no idea who I was at all.

Within a work situation I hated confrontation, took on more work than I could cope with and then felt bad when I couldn't complete it. I then felt guilty and set myself up to fail again.

I was perceived as a little girl and constantly felt I wasn't taken seriously, but then I wasn't taking myself seriously. I didn't believe that I could do anything on my own. I had to have the backing of a man to say that I could do something and when this was taken away I self destructed. I was scared to step outside of my comfort zone. In fact I didn't even know what one was.

I knew I had a lot of work to do to unravel the tangled web of my life and it felt so much easier to hide away and wallow in blaming other people, and don't get me wrong I am human and I did have my fair share of angry outbursts, but I realised afterwards that although I had expressed a deeply held emotion I hadn't actually got rid of it. I couldn't at the time cope with addressing everything in one go as it was just so huge and I would slip into overwhelm and spend hours staring blankly at a wall, so I decided to break things down into much smaller tasks. By taking a task that you avoid doing you can achieve it if you break it down into smaller and smaller tasks until it becomes so small that it becomes easy. When you achieve each one you can tick it off and go on to the next one. If you struggle on one of the tasks step back take a deep breath and break that task down until you feel you can achieve it. This can work on just about anything that you are procrastinating on, or find uncomfortable or difficult to do, and learning this will help you in many areas of your life.

Below is an example to show how this process would work.

You want to be able to go to the corner shop but you are too scared to even open the front door.

This could be how you break the task down for each day.

- I put on my shoes.

- I put on my shoes and my coat.

- I put on my shoes and my coat and pick up my keys.

- I put on my shoes and my coat and pick up my keys, and then I open the door and sit on the step for one minute.

- I put on my shoes and my coat and pick up my keys, then I open the door and sit on the step for one minute, then I walk to the end of the driveway and back.

- I put on my shoes and my coat and pick up my keys, then I open the door and sit on the step for one minute, then I walk to the end of the driveway, then I walk to the next-door neighbour's driveway and back home.

- I put on my shoes and my coat and pick up my keys, then I open the door and sit on the step for one minute, then I walk to the end of the driveway, then I walk to the next-door neighbour's driveway before continuing to the corner shop and then back home.

In this scenario maybe the sitting on the step for a minute was too difficult so just break it down into two or more steps.

- I open the door and sit on the step for one minute

Becomes

- I open the door and sit on the step for 30 seconds

- I open the door and sit on the step for one minute

The tasks can be as small as you need them to be as long as you are continually moving forward.

During this time I came across a book by Lauren Mackler entitled "Solemate – Master the Art of Aloneless & Transform Your Life" it spoke deeply to me although it took me a long time to be able to read it. I also found that " Codependent No More" by Melody Beattie, "Facing Love Addiction" by Pia Mellody and "Psychopath Free" by Jackson MacKenzie were guiding lights in my darkness and with their wealth of knowledge the first task I chose to learn was the most difficult word in the dictionary "No".

It only has two letters but it is surprisingly hard to say. I started to practice saying it in the mirror to myself and gradually as I became more comfortable with how it sounded and felt, I started to integrate it into my daily life. It wasn't a case of saying no to everything it was about being present in the moment, of connecting with your gut and recognising that feeling when someone is asking you to do something that you don't want to do, and then identifying the feeling that it brings up. I would feel a fear of abandonment, a fear of not being liked, and a fear of being hurt if I didn't say yes. This was a revelation to me because the fear wasn't about the task that was being requested. How could you have such a fear from a request to pick up a pint of milk? It boiled down to being able to put myself as an equal to those around me. I had a right to actually say no because I didn't have time or I wasn't able to do what they asked or I didn't want to and that was ok. I didn't suddenly become someone who wouldn't be helpful in anyway, I enjoyed being helpful but I instead started to check in with my gut reaction first. Did I feel happy to help or did I feel used and taken for granted? The first few times I faced my fear, I put the request into context and said no. However what I wasn't prepared for was the sudden change in request. It was rephrased to illicit a guilt response or one of my fears, I caved instantly. So recognising this I started to practice maintaining a no response no matter what. The more I practiced the easier it became and I felt better and more appreciated. I now rarely have to say no more than once because people know I'm not going to change my mind. However at the beginning I had to say it a number of times until people got the message that no meant no.

What was interesting is that the people around me started to change, some took a step closer and a lot took a step away, and although this was painful to see at first I began to realise that the ones who became closer were much better for me.

I had put in place the first tentative strands of assertiveness and I was proud of myself.

Chapter 17

Dark Night of the Soul

Much as I wanted to blame the world and his wife for every slight that had caused me to suffer, I also now had to accept my own role in prolonging my suffering, because of my own fear of change. Would it have hurt as much if I had faced my fear, got rid of the boyfriend, and got rid of the shop, as soon as it started to fail, rather than slapping on yet another plaster to avoid the pain of knowing I had put all that effort in only to walk away?

I refer to this period as the dark night of my soul. It was a period where I was forced to confront my reality and I had so many questions suddenly, and the most frustrating was why?

The time came to shut the doors permanently on the shop, I was deeply conscious of my failure to make it a success. The final day was so depressing and it was difficult not to let emotion overcome me but I managed. Admitting to myself that it wasn't going to work was especially hard to do, but I packed up what was left and stored it in the corner of my room. The final day was so depressing and it was difficult not to let emotion overcome me but I managed to hold it together. Again no-one understood how much of myself was invested in that shop and losing it just felt like another part of me was fracturing. I still found that people would change the subject or walk away rather than listen to what I was going through and I couldn't be bothered to make an effort to engage them. I was angry that I would often listen to people's most difficult times and be supportive but when the tables were turned you wouldn't see them for dust. I thought it was because they didn't care.

I had literally lost a piece of myself I didn't know who I was anymore. I had no desire to connect with anyone. I hated Facebook with a passion. It was to me at the time full of mindless drivel. If I posted my feelings I was ignored but someone posting a picture of their dinner was massively popular. I struggled to understand the complex emotions that were fighting inside. I felt a deep need for connection but couldn't bear the thought of being around anyone who would reject me or want something from me. I was hyper alert all the time terrified to trust anyone. Massively overwhelmed struggling with extreme grief and self destructive outbursts something had to give. So I searched for some therapy, someone to give me an honest opinion.

The first few times I attended I did nothing but sob uncontrollably but eventually she built up enough trust with me that we could finally prise open the box that I had been struggling to bury. Piece by piece we laid out my life and all the difficulties I had experienced. We started right from the beginning of my life and covered everything to the present day. She ripped off the bandages of the festering wounds of my soul and dug out the maggots. I have never felt so exposed but finally I was able to express how I felt verbally. For six months every week I went along to have my life ripped apart and experienced every emotion connected to every dark period of my life and there were many and I started to realise how often I had buried the feelings and never expressed them. I felt raw and vulnerable.

Chapter 18

Finding Support

The world has changed radically in the last few decades and in some ways that is great and in others it isn't. We currently have a worse connection with our fellow human beings than at any time ever before. I may be able to talk to a friend on the other side of the world by posting on social media, but actual face to face in depth mutually beneficial conversation is becoming rarer to see especially among the young.

Our self worth currently is dictated from birth by TV, magazines, celebrities and numerous corporations telling you what you need to look like, be and have. We rush to accumulate stuff, boast about where we go on holiday and strive to maintain the status quo of standing within our peer group. How many hundreds of social media friends can I get and do I have enough likes. It saddens me that when groups of people do meet they are all peering at their phones busy tweeting and sharing the moment they are sitting with their friends, rather than actually having a real conversation with the ones sitting next to them.

So if you haven't got a really close friend to use as a sounding board for your problems don't worry it is not unusual, it won't be forever. Look around for alternatives to fill the gap for now. Engaging with a therapist to untangle your thoughts and give you some clarity is a good way to go and can often resolve situations more rapidly as they can be from a neutral point of view which friends can find hard to do. Value yourself and know that you deserve help to deal with your situation. You don't have to be embarrassed they have heard all sorts of problems and nothing you say will shock or upset them.

If you can't use a therapist then seeking out a support group either online or in your town. Talking to people who are going through similar situations always helps.

Chapter 19

Edna

An Aha moment for my personal life came in the form of a shop mannequin called Edna she was the prop used by an inspirational lady called Heidi Sawyer. Heidi is the Course Director for the Institute of Psychic Development. She travels the world teaching psychic awareness and self-healing at workshops and events, and has written numerous articles and books on self-improvement and psychic development. I had gone along to watch a talk she was giving. It was one of the few places I felt calm, and I could get away from the constant arguments in my psyche. Her talk was based around how we treat ourselves with food and self destructive actions, and Edna the mannequin was being used as a stand in for herself. Although at times it was funny to see Heidi shouting at Edna the mannequin it really hit home how we often treat ourselves worse than we would treat our own worst enemy. How rarely we actually spend the time to really listen to what our inner world is trying to say.

When I got home I sat myself down and as my own friend I asked myself what do you need? And this time I listened. The answer I received was surprising it wasn't to connect or be loved it was for peace, time to heal and quiet space to find answers and to stop putting myself into situations that weren't good for me.

I posted on my Facebook of my decision to close my account and no-one questioned it. One by one I deleted everyone. For the first time in my life I had drawn a line in the dirt my first ever boundary, albeit that it was more like a hundred foot wall with machine gun turrets on the top. It was a start.

Walking away from everything was the hardest decision I have ever made but I was conscious of the need to make sense of my thoughts. I scheduled in regular times in my day so I could have a good cry and if I was having a particularly bad time I would change my work schedule to allow me time to recover. I organised myself to ensure I focused on working in manageable sections. Weekends and holidays were my worst times so I just pretended they didn't exist. I moved my working week to seven days a week and allowed myself a few hours each morning instead to read or watch a film and concentrated on getting to know myself again.

Chapter 20

Me, Myself &I

Looking after yourself is about developing a connection with you first and fore most, and becoming your own best friend.

If you could have the perfect best friend what would he or she be like? What would they say or not say? What special gifts would they share with you? How would they protect you and make you feel safe? How would they stop your self-destructive traits from manifesting and yes we all have them? How would they help you, when you were sad? How would they make you smile? You know yourself better than anyone and when things are tough you know what to do to lighten the situation. Yes you are probably already saying I would just reach for the cream cake, a bottle of vodka, a packet of cigarettes or a bet on the horses, but the difference is that this isn't about allowing your negative destructive traits to appear. Your perfect friend would recognise all of those activities as not beneficial for you, unlike a real best friend who you might be able to fool. They would distract you with good for you activities. I am not going to waste time telling you what things you should do, because you already know that. What I am going to say is that, when you reach for that cream cake, or glass of wine get your "new best friend" to ask you this question. Are you eating that cream cake because it is just something fun to do, and you could easily put it down and not eat it, or are you eating it to cover a painful emotion, caused by a recent situation that you are not talking about or dealing with? If it is the latter then try a distraction instead or look closer at what you need to do to resolve that emotion to neutral.

Your plasters can be anything from the obvious alcohol, drugs, anorexia, self-harming, and workaholic behaviours through to anger and running away. When something upsets you what do you instinctively turn to, a glass of wine? That is your plaster. It could even be co-dependent behaviour with someone close to you.

Learning to self-soothe without self destructing is what you are aiming for.

When we become aware of our self-destructive traits they often seem to manifest on a more regular basis for a while so you feel like you are not moving forward but are slipping backwards. Do not panic these are what my friend Julie affectionately calls a wobble and they happen to us all as we start to work on ourselves. Just accept that it is happening and allow the emotion to come forward. Identify what it is and what it is associated with.

You may want to shout or have a few tears but stick with it and it will soon pass. You will know you have processed and cleared the emotion from your system when the desire for that cream cake becomes you could take it or leave it instead of I have to have it right now.

By aiming to regularly empty out your personal storage box for all those moments where you didn't deal with the problem straight away, you are less likely to suffer from overwhelm and from there depression. You will also be more relaxed and happier in general regardless of your life circumstances. I now make a conscious effort to keep my box as empty as possible.

Now you have your best friend sorted you will realise that this is not a quick fix solution. We are all guilty of neglecting ourselves from time to time but it becomes a problem when it becomes all the time, right now this above pretty much anything else, is super important to get a handle on.

You are currently facing an incredibly difficult time in your life and now that you have acknowledged that, you also have to understand that it will not be a sprint to change your life for the better. It will be a marathon, and in order to have the best chance of being physically, mentally and spiritually fit when your solution appears, you have to ensure that you are in tip top condition. I mean what is the point of finally being given the best opportunity to succeed, and you are too knackered to use it.

The analogy I like to use for this is to imagine you are flying in an aeroplane, with all of the people who mean the most to you. The plane hits trouble and the oxygen masks are deployed. None of the passengers know how to put their oxygen masks on without your assistance. Currently you are running up and down the aisle putting on masks until finally you keel over from lack of oxygen. What I want to show you is, that if you put your own oxygen mask on first and look after yourself, you can lead by example and achieve far more.

What does looking after me actually look like then? It is much bigger than ordering a salad for lunch and strapping on a pair of trainers.

The body and the mind are incredibly connected and just as a problem with your mental health can produce physical symptoms so can the reverse happen. A physical symptom can produce a mental problem.

I didn't take this on board until I became unwell for two years as a direct result of the long term stress I had endured, so that is why I am highlighting it here so you don't have to be affected by it. At my worst I struggled to be able to walk from my bed to the toilet without my heart-rate going through the roof. I had to use a mobility scooter to get around and was prescribed multiple medications with some not very nice side effects. My digestive system was shot and I was in constant pain. My hair was falling out, my blood pressure and cholesterol were too high, and I was too tired to achieve anything. I was left with the offer of a heart operation and having to adjust to my new life restrictions.

Therefore after extensive research as you do on Google, it became clear to me that if the negative was true, then could not the positive be true as well. I had by a combination of factors inadvertently caused my own ill-health, by not protecting and looking after myself, therefore could I also do the reverse and improve my health. I postponed the heart operation and informed my cardiologist that I wanted to try fixing my digestive system first to see what impact it would have on my heart. He reluctantly agreed, but stated I would be back shortly begging for the heart operation, and kept my appointment open for a few more months.

If I looked after my body and my mind and gave them all the good things they needed to cope with this difficult period, then not only would my body improve, so hopefully would my mind.

There are many studies that prove that during stressful situations the body uses up or loses key vitamins and minerals. If the stress is short lived the body has stores and will be able to cope adequately. However when you undergo stress over a longer period of time and couple that, with a desire to eat comfort food to make ourselves feel better, skipping exercise and indulging in less than helpful social pursuits like drinking, then not only is the body losing key nutrients, it also isn't replacing the stores properly either. Without these it becomes difficult for the body to process other key ingredients that are important for our correctly running body. When the body gets to a key level of vitamin and mineral deficiency, then the systems in the body become damaged and are unable to work properly or an illness appears. Magnesium and B vitamins are two that I have found to be very important and both are easily lost when you are in stressful situations. As we get older we find it more difficult to absorb these vitamins anyway, but a deficiency in these can hinder your recovery and can contribute to a number of stress related illnesses.

It is important to listen to your body and look at adjusting your diet as well, and not just rely on popping vitamins to make it as easy as possible for your body to remember how to gain nutrition. So I looked at all the normal things and this time actually made an effort to implement them consistently within my life. I dramatically increased my vegetable and fruit intake. I dropped the alcohol completely. I ate smaller portions and restricted wheat to the bare minimum. I ate more fish and smaller portions of meat even going totally vegetarian for part of the week. I reduced sugar for most of the week and cut out as many processed foods as possible and even started to enjoy drinking water. Yes I still had the odd treat but it wasn't on a daily basis and that is what made the difference. After a two year NHS wait I had an operation to fix a hernia I suspected I had that turned out to be true, and along with my improved diet and gentle exercise it meant that I was able to completely turn my health around. My heart improved and with my doctor's agreement I was able to wean myself off some heavy duty medication and I no longer needed a heart operation. The other thing it did, as I had suspected, is that it improved my mental wellbeing massively. I started to notice how different I felt when I was eating things that didn't agree with my body, sluggish, bloated and down, and what those foods are will be different for each of us.

To me it is not a surprise to learn that those on the lower income scale with higher levels of stress and depression compounded by a draw to the cheaper processed comfort food options along with self-harming behaviours, will inevitably lead to them having a higher level of poor health complaints. If we as a society could just look at changing this dynamic we would have healthier, happier people regardless of what income level they had. Providing every family with good quality fruit and vegetables that are very easily affordable instead of making them more expensive than junk food, reducing the sugar content dramatically in our food, and banning dangerous artificial additives and colourings, would go a long way to helping our populations stem the epidemic tide of depression, diabetes, and heart problems that are plaguing the western world.

Obviously check with your doctor first by asking for a full blood test to check there is nothing badly deficient, but if all is ok, and with the blessing of your doctor, a good quality multi-vitamin supplement will ensure that physically you are providing your body with the optimum nutrition it so desperately needs, and filling any gaps during this stressful time. That way unlike me you won't have to suffer a physical illness as well. Just make sure you read the label to get a good balance as some multivitamins can be heavily weighted on one or two at the exclusion of the rest or the amount of one exceeds the RDA (recommended daily amount) by a very long way which can in some cases lead to toxicity in continued use. If in doubt ask advice from your pharmacy or doctor for what is the best option for you with your own unique health challenges.

We all know that we should be taking regular exercise and I am going to say that is still very important but I am going to expand on this and say the type of exercise you are doing while you are in a stressful period can both help and hinder your progress. To be able to flow through this stressful time as easily as possible you need to utilise the correct system.

The body has two systems the sympathetic nervous system, and the parasympathetic nervous system. These two systems influence a number of internal organs in the body and more importantly for this section they work in opposition to each other.

The sympathetic nervous system is more recognisable as our flight or fight system, it bursts in to action when we are in danger. In the distant past it was the system that would allow us to fight off a wild animal or run away. It increases our heart rate and raises our blood pressure and constricts our blood vessels. It also diverts attention away from mundane bodily processes such as digestion to ensure we have everything we need to survive.

The parasympathetic nervous system is the opposite. It reduces the heart rate, lowers blood pressure, relaxes the blood vessels, promoting a rest and relax approach. It focuses on digestion and waste removal.

When we are not stressed, either mentally, physically or emotionally then these systems work nicely together. We spend a lot of our time using the parasympathetic system with short bursts with the sympathetic system which is activated by hormones.

When we are in difficult situations we spend a bigger proportion of time in our sympathetic system which means we are using up more key nutrients in order to stay alert. We have more stress on our organs and less recovery time combined with less efficient digestion and waste removal which in the long term will make us feel rubbish. Then to add to this we decide that it is a great idea to pound away on the running track. Go for the burn at intense aerobic activities or weightlifting.

What does this achieve? Our bodies don't understand that we are not running away from a wild animal they think we are, due to the increase in hormones. Our sympathetic system is firing away, so not only are we stressed by what life is throwing at us we are expanding that stress by adding it to our workout routine.

If you spend the majority of your life in your parasympathetic system then yes short bursts of intense exercise are great but if you are in a stressful situation you want to help your body to flip the switch and get more into its parasympathetic system. You need to be doing gentle exercise, Yoga, Tai chi, gentle walking or swimming. Any activity you can do and still comfortably hold a conversation or breathe through your nose.

By doing gentle exercise for just thirty minutes a day you will be encouraging your body to relax and reduce stress which will improve your digestion and waste removal processes.

If for health reasons you struggle with exercise then concentrate on learning to breathe better. If you can get outside and face the wind then do, or if not look out of a window or look at a nature picture. Just take a moment to fill your lungs and breathe in and out slowly for a few minutes a day. When we are stressed we tend to breathe very shallowly and over time the body gets used to not taking proper breaths. Even just doing this for a few weeks you will notice a difference in how you feel.

Hopefully by now you have had a little go at meditation and have seen some of the benefits of keeping your negative mind chatter under control, so now it is also worth mentioning that you also need to be aware of what is good in your life, so that you can be aware of new good things.

I am sure it has happened to you in the past, but say you bought a new car you would suddenly be seeing that make, model and colour everywhere, when before you hadn't seen one. If you are a woman, and you find yourself pregnant you will find every other woman you walk past is pregnant too. It isn't the world conspiring against you, it is just that your brain is aware of millions of pieces of information a day but it only serves up those bits of information that are important to you, based on your thoughts. Therefore if you are only thinking depressive, self-defeating thoughts, that is exactly what your brain is going to flag up for you to notice, regardless of the fact that there are many more positive things to notice. So instead become grateful for even the small things, and consciously notice them, then your brain will look for similar things around you to flag up for you to notice too. Try it with coins or feathers on the ground, every time you see one pick it up say thank you and put it in your pocket. You will be surprised how many you start to find. I was so guilty of not noticing good things in the past. I honestly took a lot of things for granted, and didn't appreciate them. When I was experiencing some of my toughest times there were still things that I should have taken joy in.

So take the time to notice. I spent almost a year while I was ill not being able to walk very far anywhere. Recently after I had recovered I caught myself being annoyed that I didn't have enough money to put diesel in my car which meant I would have to walk to town when it was starting to rain. I stopped and pulled myself up on it realising how lucky I was to be able to now walk the one mile to the town and back which I couldn't have done a year ago. Not having the diesel money and walking in the rain didn't matter anymore, and I literally glided to the shops with a massive grin on my face grateful that it was something I could now do. Although it probably freaked a few people out as I walked past.

It is not until we lose something that we appreciate what we had and we are all at some point going to experience the loss of someone or something. Don't wait to lose it before you appreciate having it or them in your life. Even during the devastating loss of a loved one, remember to appreciate the loved ones you still have in your life. I now have a fantastic network of family and friends around me who I truly value and a job I love and the time to write when and what I want. I live by the sea and the joy I feel being able to walk along the sea front, feel the wind in my hair and sit and watch the waves is amazing. No I can't quite go for a jog yet, buy a new outfit, or take my family out for a meal, but I refuse to dwell on what I can't do today and instead I engage with what I have got and what I can do. The more I am grateful for a sunny day, a cool breeze, a stranger's smile, the better I feel and the more happiness I bring to those I come into contact with and that in turn makes me happy too.

Every day I see all the little improvements that my change in mental attitude is bringing towards me and it makes me so excited to see my new life unfolding around me. So give it a try. Yes things are bad for you right now but what have you got in your life you aren't taking notice of?

Chapter 21

The Golden Nugget

Life gradually started to stabilise slowly. The shop was finally closed down and the remaining stock was sold off. Sad as I was at its demise I was also now grateful for all the important life lessons I had learnt along the journey.

I had incorporated a regular routine of rest and relaxation along with gentle exercise. I was thoroughly enjoying my daily brisk strolls along the sea-front in the bracing sea air.

I practiced meditation and had resolved many issues in my relationships, finally I was able to start writing the long thought of book that was still pricking my conscious.

Probably in common with most ideas I had a time of starting and stopping before throwing it all away and starting again but above all I knew I had to keep trying to write what was in my head on to paper I think it is probably something all authors struggle with at times. I was keen to prove myself

I had been on a quest to improve my ability to network. To be honest I was rubbish, I got nervous and sweaty before I said anything and got a massive frog in my throat as soon as I started to speak. But I had been doing a lot of self-improvement so I bit the bullet and started attending some of the free courses that cluttered my email inbox. Normally run by super successful millionaires they are actually really interesting topics, and always provide a few golden nuggets of information for free, that you can use when you get back to real life.

The key as I worked out expensively early on is to leave your credit card at home. The selling is so perfectly done that people are literally running to the back of the room waving their credit cards to sign up, which is great if you have money but not so good if you are worried you won't have the train fare home. Yes I was in the second camp there. I enjoyed going though because it gave me the opportunity to practice chatting to people while I learned and eventually I worked up the courage to actually talk to the super successful speaker.

The first time it was general chit chat about the day but gradually each time I stepped a little further until finally D-day had arrived, and I clumsily presented the idea for my book and a quick outline of what it would contain.

James MacNeil was my man he had made a fantastic presentation that had so inspired me. James is a super successful person who has coached thousands of people and among many other things is the author of the best-selling book "The Guru builder".

If you ever get a chance to see him or attend one of his courses you will not be disappointed. I stood like a panic-stricken goldfish opening and closing my mouth and to his absolute credit he pretended not to notice. He said he liked the cover and it sounded like it could be an interesting book and gave me some encouraging tips. He said, once I had finished the book I should get in touch with his team, who would be able to help further.

I was thrilled a super successful author liked me. He thought I was good enough. I was so excited. My imagination took off like a rocket. In my mind I was already watching Lorries full of my book, arriving at WH Smiths.

The high lasted for a full month until buoyed by my recent success I aimed to get more authors involved in "Okaying" my book still before I had really begun it properly. Damian Mark Smyth author of "How to be Stress Free in 24 Hours!" and Tony Stockwell author of "Walking with Angels" were the next people I met and they were amazing guys and so accommodating in providing me with advice and encouragement. I eagerly wrote a few more chapters until fate conspired to put me into the path of a certain multi-millionaire who for the purpose of this narrative will remain unnamed.

I had actually paid for this particular course that I was attending, and it was held over a few days chock full of really valuable content. It was towards the end of the morning session and I was buzzing with great ideas. Break was called and the aforementioned unnamed multi-millionaire hovered by the stage near my table, so I took the opportunity to show him my book cover and a quick sentence on the proposed content. He said it wasn't something he really wanted to go into now and suggested that I talk to a member of his team. Not overly upset by the interaction I retired for some refreshments before the next session. It was literally over in a couple of minutes and that included a photo of him and me together.

I took my seat again at my table ready for the next session, pen poised to record the golden nuggets due to pour from his lips. I was eager to get as much value for my hard earned money as I could. Without even hesitating the unnamed multi-millionaire chose to announce to all of the couple of hundred people in the room that he had been approached during the break by a lady who had shown him her book cover. He proceeded to rant about how unprofessional it was and how could she possibly think it was ok to approach him, and about how he was a much better author. He to save embarrassing her obviously didn't want to name her so he wouldn't.

My face burned a bright crimson. I was sitting on the round table close to the stage on the left-hand-side. Every-one on my table knew that I was producing a book, as we had chatted about it and their own business ideas over tea and biscuits as part of the course and he knew that. People on the nearest tables started to look at me and I felt like I wanted the ground to open up and swallow me. My palms were sweaty and my heart was racing. Why hadn't he said, No when I asked if he could take a quick look at my book cover? I wanted to get up and run from the room. But I didn't dare move. I wasn't going to give him the satisfaction of seeing me leave. That and the rest of room would definitely have known who he was talking about. I felt sick to the pit of my stomach and I could visibly feel people cringing around me. It probably only lasted for ten minutes but it felt like hours to me. I couldn't wait for the lunch break and none of what he said for the next hour registered in my shocked brain.

Lunch break finally arrived and I quickly left the room. Person after person came up to me to check I was ok. Many saying they were shocked by how brutal he had been. Lunch ended and with that all my confidence did too. I couldn't face going back into the lecture room. Finally defeated as the last person left the lunch area, I hid in the corner and had a few tears. I didn't want to write anymore I obviously wasn't that good. I was stupid, an idiot and lots of other negative comments. I felt hurt and angry and like a piece of pooh on the sole of his shoe.

I was contemplating packing up and leaving to go home, when one of his team appeared a lovely young girl. She offered me a tissue and listened patiently while I explained what had happened, and with the retelling of the story it became clear that I had been making a terrible mistake all along. I had literally allowed a toxic person to charge unchecked straight into my inner circle. I had placed all of my own self-worth on people I didn't even know. I hadn't thought about whether I felt good enough, whether I liked my book or even if I thought it was a good topic, and for the first few people I had been lucky that they were self-aware enough to be able to encourage and nurture me. However eventually with the luck of the draw you are going to come across someone who finds it fun to destroy instead of create.

The lesson I learnt that day was that the only person who mattered in evaluating whether I was good enough was me. No other person's view should replace your own belief in yourself and what you can achieve. Other people's opinions can be used to enhance your offering but your own belief should always make up that strong unbreakable foundation. Then no matter what difficult people you meet, who have their own unknown agenda, you will be able to shrug it off and continue your journey. Doing the book was never about massaging my own ego it had always been just a fulfilment of a promise, a special promise I had made to myself when I was homeless. I had promised that even though I was facing a truly awful time that eventually, I would write this book on how I survived. It was a book that I had wanted to be available when I was struggling. I wanted others who came after me, facing similar personal struggles, to know they weren't alone in their fight and that with perseverance things would improve, just like they had for me. I wanted my book to be that light in the dark if someone needed it. It didn't really matter if not one person liked it as long as I did. Providing I gave it my best shot and put it out there I could be proud of what I had achieved and that was all that mattered.

So did I go back into the lecture or did I pack up and leave?

You bet I went back into the lecture noisily twenty minutes late which momentarily disrupted the lecture, with my head held high. I am good enough and no multi-millionaire is going to make me believe any different, and that was the most valuable golden nugget of information I received that day.

Chapter 22

Climbing the Mountain

I finally felt that life was going my way. It was November 2016 and even though it had taken what felt like an eternity to write it the book was complete and ready to be self-published on Amazon.

I was so nervous and incredibly excited but with a launch of nervous energy the button was pressed and I became for the first time in my life a published author.

I was a bundle of insecurities but following the advice from my own book I concentrated on being proud of my achievement and allowing other people to have their own opinions.

Over a hundred people downloaded the book and I was thrilled. Although most of them were free downloads I had actually made a couple of quid too.

People were interested in what I was saying and I got a few nice reviews. It wasn't a best seller but it wasn't ever supposed to be. I felt like I had achieved what I had set out to do. I was looking forward to promoting the book and helping some more people to climb their own mountains.

What I didn't realise was that in a couple of short months my life was going to be in danger and I was going to hit another large dip in the road. Then the person most in need of my book was going to be me.

Chapter 23

Tea with a Psychopath

The weak wintry sun filtered through the fluffy white clouds as I joined him by the communal front door at exactly nine o'clock in the morning for the short walk to the bottom of the road. He was my new neighbour who lived in the room above me. From the moment I had first met him I had felt on edge and had tried to be polite but distant. He constantly seemed to be around and if I was paranoid I would almost say deliberately so. He had even jokingly stated that I was stalking him. I pulled my warm winter coat around me and aimed to retreat further into its comforting embrace, further from the icy chill of the north wind whistling around me. I needed to set him straight.

He was as usual irritatingly chipper but with a stark coldness to his banal banter that stabbed deep into my insides. I just felt that he wasn't being totally honest. He was a number of years older than me with a slightly gregarious manner and every time he smiled at me I noted the smile still fell disturbingly short of his eyes. He was overtly good at hurtful comments that were suddenly transformed into obvious jokes. Everything he said just felt off and he made me feel very wary. There was no doubting the warning signs I was receiving. I was looking forward to having the situation resolved so I could get on with my life promoting my book, rather than constantly feeling on guard whenever he appeared. I didn't want to create a bad atmosphere as we had to share communal areas so I had grudgingly agreed to a coffee that I paid for in a public place rather than his room. Once he truly realised that I was brutally honest about not being interested in his romantic flirtations I was sure he would find an alternative focus and leave me alone. Just being this close to him put my teeth on edge and I was struggling in my attempts to respond to superfluous small talk until we got to the cafe.

The sea came into view before us, soft foamy waves gently caressing the deserted beach. Sea gulls cawing circled high above delighting in the air currents wafting them higher and higher before releasing them to dive spectacularly down again.

Nestled in amongst the scenery was the destination for this encounter a smart beach front cafe consisting of a small section with a few white plastic tables that overhung the waves. It was a friendly relaxing venue with a complimentary blanket to keep your legs warm if you were a little chilly and I often enjoyed sitting there with a cup of tea watching the sea gulls bobbing about on the surf. It was the closest public area to my multiple occupancy property and less than a minute from where we lived. I was eager to get inside so I could face him with a table between us and other people around. Having him at my side while we walked deeply unnerved me for some reason.

The worn black and white sign on the cafe still read closed but without hesitation he reached for the door handle and pulled opened the door. Arrogantly flicking the sign from closed to open he ushered me through. The mature waitress surprised, quickly composed her expression, clearly annoyed that she had been forced into serving before she was totally ready.

Politely I requested a table for two smiling apologetically winning the waitress back on side as we briefly exchanged a look of understanding about men. She led us over to a neatly set table and we slid into our seats before ordering our drinks.

Sitting opposite him I watched the lack of expression on his face, carefully measured reactions and the lack of feeling in his eyes. I had never seen anything like it. His gaze was lazy almost hypnotic like the eyes of snake with a dangerous edge. And I had the disconcerting impression that I was being sized up as food.

Our drinks arrived so shaking off the weird feeling I gathered my errant thoughts and ploughed forward with the objective of letting him down gently but effectively. He smiled revealing far too many teeth and laughed in a derogatory manner as though I was a silly school girl rather than the forty plus woman that I was. Waving a dismissive hand in the air, he said he already knew that. Then why the continual harassment then I thought. He continued to subtly put me down verbally, while still appearing overly relaxed. I recognised the toxic behaviour immediately and carefully filed it outside my inner circle so I could objectively review its content without it affecting me emotionally. His reaction wasn't what I was expecting. Upset possibly, annoyed maybe or apologetic even but not like this was some big game he was playing that I wasn't aware of.

Pinning me to my chair with a stare he flippantly asked what it was about him that I didn't like. Annoyed that he wasn't taking the hint I recklessly laid my cards on the table and threw back that I didn't trust him and that he wasn't being honest about who he was. As soon as I said it I knew I had made a big mistake.

Clearly stunned at my perception he paused, a moment of almost grudging respect filtered through his eyes. A strange feeling that this girl wasn't going to be a complete pushover seeped into my conscious. My stomach clenched uncomfortably in warning. My words hung in the frigid air between us. This guy clearly had a severely toxic if not psychopathic personality and I needed to be free of him as soon as possible.

Hastily planning my departure I shifted in my plastic seat uncomfortably, hoping that I had achieved my goal but realising, as the measured silence continued that I had instead thrown down a challenge. Noticing my covert manoeuvre he suddenly leant forward over the small table and closed the gap between us effectively forcing me out of politeness in a public place to resume the seat that I had barely left. Trapped he looked probingly into my eyes and said that he would tell me the truth then. The malice within them was plain to see. Caught on a back foot I struggled desperate to not be his confidant, aware that this was a line that I didn't want to cross. Over and over he tried to bait me, and still I said I wasn't interested in hearing. Hoping I could bring the conversation to a close, so that I could finally leave. Until suddenly he just blurted out his devastating secret. He had just been released from a thirty year sentence for murder.

Time stood still as my brain frantically absorbed the information. Ice water followed through my veins. Don't let him see you react, pounded through my mind with an urgency that took my breath away.

Impassively I returned his gaze careful to show no emotion at his revelation. Was it a game to frighten me, and he would laugh at my gullibility again, or was I sitting drinking tea with a convicted murderer?

Around us life went on as usual. The waitress shuffled past clutching some menus for the new table of diners that had just arrived. The Kitchen Staff were banging trays of food on the counter. I could hear the tinkling laughter of the elderly lady in the far corner as she was gently wrapped in the warm complimentary blanket, by her fussing daughter, at her table by the seaside window.

Only in my small area of the world had things taken a dangerous turn.

Clearly surprised by my lack of reaction, he launched into how there was something wrong with the man's brain and how he had practically begged him to help him. Desperate to be wrong about the guy sat in front of me, that sanity did still exist, my mind searched for a more palatable result. Had it been an accident? Maybe he was a brain surgeon and an operation had gone wrong? He laughed at my conclusion and seeing his opportunity chastised me for being a silly little girl. Before telling with great artistic flair how much he had enjoyed smashing his victim's head in with a hammer, although he had put him out of his misery quickly.

"If the psychiatrists knew how I really think," he said, "they'd never let me out of prison again."

True horror the like of which I have never experienced before gripped me but still I kept my face as dismissive as possible. Every muscle in my body ached at the effort not to react to what he was saying. The excitement of re-living his crime in every gory shocking Technicolor detail was evident in his animated body language. No longer was there the feeling that he wasn't being honest. Every fibre in my being was silently screaming it was the truth and there was only one reason he was telling me. He wanted to see my fear.

Knowing with absolute certainty that if I left now, I could be in imminent danger because he was so hyped up on his kill, I calmly ordered another round of drinks for us and prepared to wait out his excitement surge. It was clear to me from listening to him, that his enjoyment came from watching the fear and distress in his victim. Now whether that meant he would be happy to just frighten me, or he would want to do me harm, was not clear. My goal now, I realised was to make myself as boring as possible until I had a chance to get away.

Gradually I steered the conversation to more mundane topics, the weather, our landlord and his occupation until he became bored with trying to get me to react to his shocking revelations.

The cafe had in the interim started to fill with more and more would be diners. I toyed with the idea of leaping from my seat and begging them for help but what would I say, he hadn't done anything other than sit and drink his coffee. It was hardly a crime of the century. Eventually I realised after the disapproving stare from the waitress that I couldn't stall much longer over a cold cup of tea. I had to leave. Peering through the steamy window I was pleased to note that the sunny promenade was much busier than it had been on our walk down. Lots of families with young children in tow, dog walkers and the occasional late morning jogger in their garish Lycra shorts and obligatory plastic water bottle filled the sea-front.

He was a slight man and although taller than me he was in good physical condition. On a one minute walk would I be able to hold my own if he tried to attack me, when I was still recovering from my surgery? Would one of the pedestrians come to my aid? It was now or never.

Announcing I had a job interview that I had to attend in a few minutes I made my excuses thanked him for his company and stood up.

Paying the bill with sweaty palms and a racing heart I was disconcerted when he fell into step beside me, saying he had forgotten his key for the communal front door and he would accompany me back to the house instead.

The icy sea wind whipped at my face as I reluctantly pushed the heavy cafe door open. Choosing my route to be in front of the CCTV cameras along the front as much as I could I started on the short walk home.

Strolling alongside me he attempted to fling his arm around my shoulders but I was ready and with a loud "No", that attracted the attention of a passerby, I sidestepped him.

He laughed and gave up saying he was only joking.

After what felt like an hour we arrived at our house. Other residents were coming and going and finally I was able to slip quickly away into my room and lock the door.

For hours and hours my mind argued with itself. Was I at risk or was I over reacting? Was this guy dangerous or was it all a lie. Turning to Google I put in the name I had seen on his post but nothing came up. Surely then he was just playing a sick mind game. If he had been convicted of murder it would be all over Google somewhere. I started to relax a little but I barricaded the flimsy door with my chair though just in case. Finally in the early hours of the morning I vowed to pop into the police station to get their opinion first thing in the morning. Exhausted I fell into a deep sleep.

Chapter 24

Who Bluffs Best Survives

The golden sunlight filtered through my aging blinds caressing my sleepy eyelids, gently encouraging wakefulness. I stretched leisurely underneath my toasty warm covers my mind still entwined in slumberous strands of safety.

Suddenly a loud clatter sounded from the communal shower room next-door to my room followed by a terribly distinctive voice. My body froze in fear. He was in the shower room next to my room, moving the cleaning equipment around. My brief sleepy relaxed state had been rudely trashed. Reaching quickly for my phone I noted that I had over slept. Gone was my window of time where he would be asleep and I could slip away un-noticed. I chastised myself for not setting the alarm but I hadn't wanted the sound of it to alert him to my trip to the police station. Gently I plugged my phone in to ensure it had a full charge for when I needed it, noting as usual the persistent 'no service' that always plagued my phone unless I was outside the building. Never had having a phone I could actually use been more important than now, rather than before when it was just a minor chilly annoyance.

His cheery tones filtered through the wall. Why was he in my shower? Only I and two other residents who lived on this floor used that one. He had a number of showers to use on his own floor and had no reason to be on my floor at all.

Dread settled in the pit of my stomach. I didn't dare make a sound hoping he would think I had gone out already. My other housemates were already long gone with their work schedules. I was conscious that the Police would probably think I was wasting their time but even that guilt didn't stop the thought that something felt very, very wrong. Even if they laughed at me or locked me up I still needed to get their reassurance that I wasn't in any danger and that my neighbour was just a harmless weirdo, who liked to try and scare women.

I had slept fully clothed the night before so quietly I pulled on some clean clothes, noticing worriedly the scars on my stomach from my recent surgery as I dressed. Then I sank carefully into the chair propped up against my door barely daring to breath. My ear pressed close to the smooth painted surface I listened as he wandered loudly in and out of the shower room next-door and up and down my corridor. What was he doing?

Hour upon hour crawled past until finally there was complete silence. Nervously I still waited needing to be sure that he had indeed gone. Finally the window of opportunity I felt had arrived. He had obviously assumed I had gone out and had given up on his ploy to confront me in the shower room. I breathed a shaky sigh of relief. Rapidly I gathered my keys, phone and hand bag. Realising that I needed to have my hands free and be unrestricted just in case. I transferred what I needed to my pocket instead and the rest I put in a shopping cart. In a worse-case scenario I could use it to trip him up. Running wasn't an option due to my recent operation but I was sure I could move quickly if forced too. Pleased with my rudimentary preparations and with still no sound from beyond my door I felt confident that the time was right for my escape so I opened my front door......

Silently he stood leaning against the door frame of the doorway at the end of my corridor waiting for me, lazily swinging a claw hammer in his right hand.

Trapped I realised my error.....

My mind spun and leapt into warp speed assessing the dire situation. The corridor from my room ended at the door he was currently standing in. Only two doors other than my own led off the corridor and both of them led into a shower-room with no other exit from either.

The dim lighting flickered fitfully sending an eerie glow that bounced off the fading wallpaper even though it was the middle of the day. The lone cream painted radiator clicked loudly between us as further warm water flooded the system. The house empty of all other occupants was for once deathly quiet and my breathing seemed unusually loud in the confined space.

If I retreated back into my room I knew he would realise he had been rumbled. My weak door would only hold for a few minutes of sustained attack by that hammer and with a crowded room full of my possessions and furniture I had little room for evasion. With no phone signal and no exit from the back garden if I even managed to squeeze through the first floor window in time, going back into my room was suicidal.

In a flash I realised that my best option was to continue as I had the day before feigning total ignorance to his motives and aiming to get out of the corridor to a better more open position before he realised.

Plastering a friendly smile on my face I gave him a cheery greeting. I shut the door unwillingly behind me and pushed my shopping cart purposely in front of me down the narrow corridor directly towards him.

Caught off guard by my strange reaction he stepped back from the door clearly calculating whether he'd made it obvious enough I was in danger as I wasn't panicking, screaming and trying to slam the door in his face. The shopping cart and the narrow corridor provided the distance I needed and despite his attempts to hold open the door with his left hand and usher me through in front of him. He was instead forced through the door in front of my shopping cart to avoid being run over.

A wide flight of stairs descended to the ground floor. Keeping up a conversation about the cleaning and the errant washing machines I noticed he would purposely stop every couple of steps hoping I would continue past him and when this failed he more obviously tried to walk back up a few steps to get behind me. Drawing his attention to things in our conversation I quickly corrected our positions so I was behind or above him.

The internal male voice inside my head was practically deafening, don't turn your back to him. Keep face on and your shopping cart between you. Keep talking.

I felt like we were doing a warped kind of ballroom dance as I spun and paused and tried to herd him unobtrusively down the worn stairs before me.

The shiny hammer swung more menacingly from his hand just in the corner of my vision. I knew instinctively that if I brought attention to it that, would be his cue to use it. So I pretended not to notice it and his movements became more obvious, trying to catch my attention with its deadly silver head and black rubber handle.

With relief we finally made it through the front door and on to the pathway that led to the pavement. Here there would be plenty of other people surely to help me. But no I wasn't to find assistance there. The whole road was empty not another soul was anywhere in sight.

My breath caught in my throat and cold sweat rolled down my back. In obvious excitement and with a flourish he flung open the lid of the large industrial bin that stood by the pathway. Come and have a look inside he cajoled "I've been cleaning it out all day," beckoning for me to come and stand by his right side. Instead I carefully sidestepped keeping the bin firmly between the two of us and making sure not to lean forward to view his handy work.

A barrage of thoughts flooded my mind. Why would you clean a bin with a hammer? Why clean the bin when the bin company does it anyway? Where was the rubbish that was supposed to be in it?

The stress was starting to get to me. My heart rate was increasing. Taking a deep breath I tried to slow my breathing and get my anxiety under control.

Drawing my attention to the other side of the road he pointed out a huge pile of rubbish and berated the neighbours for making such an appalling mess. Standing to his left side I could see the hammer was getting higher and held steady. He was now holding it out from his body in a ready to swing stance.

Slowly we circled down the pathway towards the pavement with me paying special attention to keep face on to him. His excitement hung thick in the air. You could practically feel the electrical charge in the air.

By luck rather than judgement I eventually ended up with my back to the pavement and him on the pathway in front of me. Annoyance clearly etched across his face as he realised that I was getting further away from where he wanted me to be. Still there was no one in view to help me.

The hammer rose slightly higher and further out of my line of vision so that if I was to look at it I would have to turn my head. Instead I looked him in the eye. Pain coursed through my solar plexus as my muscles involuntarily knotted frantically warning me of the danger.

Suddenly with an out of body flash I could see myself kneeling over my own body in the bottom of the bin. Blood matted my long brown hair from a gaping head wound and my eyes still open staring blankly away. The sheer excitement of my kill coursed through my body producing an almost unbelievable deranged high while the metallic smell of blood still hung warm in the frigid air.

Slamming back into reality I could see he was advancing towards me. My mind was still working at the speed of light. Hastily holding his gaze resolutely, I told him I would be back in a couple of hours to continue our conversation. My friend, I said was waiting at the top of the road for me and if I didn't get there soon he would come looking for me.

Pausing for reflection I could see he was considering whether he had enough time. Finding that he might not and that I might be telling the truth about my friend, a cocky smile rapidly replaced the previous annoyance. The cheery manner reappeared. The hammer dropped to his side and he backed a few steps away. Taking the time to ensure I was coming back and that we could resume our conversation but this time in his room. He stood and deliberately watched me cross the road and walk slowly all the way up the road and round the corner.

Chapter 25

Trust Your Gut

If you only read one page within this book then this is the page you should read. We go through life day to day until one day we might be confronted with a life threatening situation. What you do during that moment can make the difference and I always feel that being prepared before an event like that happens to you or a loved one may give you the edge in surviving when the world kicks you hard in the teeth.

Throughout my life I have had opportunities where I have received a gut feeling about something or someone and at the beginning I dismissed them and always had reason to regret that decision. However as I grew older I chose to embrace my sensitivity instead. Science is still working to prove or disprove this, but to me that is not important. I feel that your gut intuition is hardwired into our bodies to provide an emergency red flag system when there is a threat to our safety. It bypasses the brain and hits you right in the solar plexus. The more dangerous the threat the stronger the sensation is. This could be physical, financial, mental, emotional or spiritual. This would be great if it wasn't for societal conventions that war with that inner knowledge that we are sensing. Often we ignore that information because we feel silly or there is no evidence to back the feeling up at that point. We haven't the courage to face the situation or the loss of something if our intuition turns out to be right.

Firstly I feel that at the least you should acknowledge that message, just accept that something in your life isn't right. Don't ignore it. Thank your intuition for bringing that information to your attention and then pay attention to how you feel after and to what this information is attached to. At the very least doing that could save your life in a serious situation.

So what do you do in a serious life threatening situation? Firstly become aware of your surroundings and any escape options. In confrontation situations you don't have to be obvious that you are looking around. Relax and look out of the corner of your eye. Look into shop windows, car mirrors or any reflective surface. Look at the shadows. Get your hands free. Move gradually to a better position if you are able to. Hide.

If you can then you should ask for help. Don't put yourself in danger by not wanting to appear silly for over-reacting. If your gut is telling you that you are in danger then you probably are. Always put your personal safety above any worries that people won't take you seriously. I didn't in the cafe and instead risked my life walking back to my home with a convicted killer just because I didn't want to make a fuss. Do not make the same mistake as you may not get a second chance. Predators rely on their prey discounting how much danger they are in.

Stay as calm as you can. Try and breathe deeply and slowly. The natural response is to panic and to breathe quicker flooding your system with adrenaline. This has its place in a fighting or running situation but it doesn't last long. In order to assess your situation and options you need to engage the more logical side of your brain and be able to listen to your intuition which will be harder to do if you have loads of adrenaline coursing through your veins.

If your potential attacker will let you, talk to him. Keep calm and try not to appear scared. Avoid him for as long as possible. Smile and look him in the eye and if you have to then lie, whatever it takes to be able to get away to safety.

If the threat of violence is imminently on the cards and you can't avoid it, and especially if you are a woman facing a man, then strike first as fast as possible and then run. We all have this action hero mentality that we will deftly avoid the bad guy's first punch and then we will honourably retaliate. But in real life it never goes that way. We end up freezing, hurt or disorientated, so get in first, make a lot of noise, shout and attack quickly. The best outcome will be you shock him and he hesitates to continue coming after you giving you precious time to get away. Learning self defence so you are prepared in advance is always a good idea too.

When we are faced with less immediate threats to our safety similar principles should be followed. Breathe, assess your situation, and then investigate to get further information, acknowledge your own worries of dealing with the situation. By taking action to resolve the situation calmly rather than waiting and reacting negatively when you are forced to, any upset will be minimised.

For example the breakup of a relationship is easier to deal with if you have put in place a good network of friends to support you through the break up rather than sitting alone watching him pack a suitcase. Losing your job is easier to deal with if you have already been looking for a new job or taken steps to reduce your financial outlay before it happens, rather than waving a P45 at your shocked wife. Don't look at your gut feelings as only bad news look at them as a tool to help you glide through the more difficult moments of your life. A signal to get your ship in order before the storm hits.

Sometimes you may be able to avoid the situation your intuition warned you about entirely and other times you may unfortunately still have to go through some of the situation, however by being prepared and listening to your intuition you will be better placed to come through the other side with the minimum of damage and ready to bounce back to good times when the circumstances present themselves. No matter how awful a situation is there is always a special insight that we gain if we look hard and long enough. Never give up fighting.

Chapter 26

Psychopathic Hangover

My psychopath was arrested and was found to have an extensive violent past including being convicted of murder. It was believed that he was stalking me and did intend to do me harm and was taken to court. My ex-boyfriend was surprisingly helpful during the court case. He was unfazed by the emotion of the situation and his calm demeanour enabled me to settle my terrified thoughts and engage the logical practical side of my brain. Although I often wanted to seek his support for my emotional needs I was very careful not to rely on him on any level and sought out more emotionally supportive people. My decision was proved correct when he admitted that the Police had asked how I was and he had realised that he hadn't a clue as he had forgotten to ask. When I laughed at that guilty omission I knew I was truly over him.

Although my psychopath stood trial, no conviction could be made due to insufficient evidence. This had a devastating effect on my health and wellbeing in the following months. I was overnight made homeless again as it was deemed I was in imminent danger by the police. I was diagnosed with post traumatic stress disorder and as a direct result my fragile self-employment after my two years of ill-health collapsed completely. I was left homeless, bankrupt, and without employment suffering panic attacks. I took down my newly published book scared to have it in print in case he found me and retreated into waiting for the mental health system to grind slowly into life.

For months I suffered scared to see anyone or be anywhere, waiting, until finally I met Chris my therapist. He was a lovely guy and over the precious few weeks the mental health system allocated me, he endeavoured to help me with my PTSD. However with the added problem of the delays in resolving my housing and finances issues, I made some progress but not enough. During our sessions I had mentioned this book and he had asked to read it so he could see where I was mentally before the incident so he could help me. On our last session I was acutely aware that I wasn't ready to give up therapy. I was firmly in the belief system again that I wanted someone else to fix my problems, looking for that man on a pedestal to save me. So I just said to him. "Chris I wish there was a map that I could use to get out of this situation." I thought that he would wave a proverbial magic wand, and a new version of therapy would appear that would fix all my problems, so I didn't have to. He instead smiled and looked me in the eye, "There is and you wrote it". Stunned into silence I just looked at him before realising that after the incident I had fallen back into bad patterns. I wasn't doing any of the self care I had spent so long learning and writing about. So I gave myself an internal hug and forgave myself for slipping back into those bad habits.

Alone once more, I opened my book and as my tears fell, I started to read and step by step I reminded myself of all the strategies that I had forgotten. Sometimes taking a step back leads to taking an even bigger step forward.

Chapter 27

Happy Ever After

I for a long time put off writing this book because I originally believed that I had to have my life fixed and be super successful before I could write about it. I mean who would want to hear from me, but I was wrong. At the time I was going through my dark times I wanted there to be a book just like this one, by anyone, so I could just for a moment not feel so alone. During my journey and many conversations it became apparent that I wasn't the only one to feel this way. So don't feel you need to be at a certain level before you share your light you don't, just share it anyway. If life throws you a curve ball like it did me after I published my book the first time you just share your light again knowing that just like last time it is just a dip in the road of life and you will soon be climbing the mountain to the summit again.

I have read many books from super successful people and I always ended up with the same question. What did they do when they had absolutely nothing, like me, that made the difference and got them back on the right road?

I understood that they had invested time and money in themselves. They got a lucky break or they worked hard. They got promoted, or took a chance, or had a positive mindset, but always it felt like they started from slightly above where I was now, and I could never work out the missing part to get me from here to that level, and by the time they got around to writing their memoirs they couldn't really remember all the intricate details, or even exactly where those first steps had even started from.

This book then tries to fill that gap. It is those first few mental steps to get you going in the right direction. It is for you if you are living on the street, it is for you if you are depressed, it is for you if you have lost absolutely everything, it is for you if you are facing bankruptcy, or been kicked in the teeth by a relationship, and you have tried so hard that you just want to give up. Always remember to keep fighting you never know how very, very close you are to success when you throw in the towel.

I spent quite a while totally focused on finding out about myself. It was tough at times but what I found was more than worth it. I learnt how to have proper useful boundaries with people that were neither too high nor too low. I made mistakes along the way, as we all do, but I now have a fantastic supportive group of friends and family that like me for being me.

I am no longer afraid to be me. If people don't like that then I am happy to let them leave my life. I am no longer willing to compromise who I am to fit what someone else thought I should be. I am finally able to be happy just following my own path whether that is alone, or in company.

I appreciate the wonder of life and the beauty of nature and I take the time to notice what is around me and I am grateful for the opportunities that I am being continually presented with.

I am able to look after myself physically, mentally, emotionally and spiritually and make sure all my needs are balanced equally.

There have been numerous points in my life that have been a challenge, and there will probably be more in the future, but they are also my greatest teachers and as horrific as it was at times, I wouldn't have changed the experience for anything. I am grateful for having endured it, so never berate yourself if you take a temporary slide backwards. Without them I would not have developed the strength and passion to be the person I am now. I am no longer afraid to follow my heart and my intuition wherever they might lead. My life is back on track and getting better every day. I am happy and healthy with a beautiful new home and financially things continue to improve. Life is pretty awesome.

If I can do that, then so can you........

I also took the opportunity before I re-published this book to add a few new bits to the original book. My own special insight if you will after the most recent experience.

When you have a dream and life throws crap in the way, don't give up. Just believe that you can achieve it no matter what, and soon you will.

For me not even a psychopathic murderer or a grumpy multi-millionaire can stop this book from being out there, and I don't know any other author who can say that.

Acknowledgments

My Family

The love and support through all the tough times I can never hope to repay. I love you all loads and loads.

My Friends

Thank you to all of you for your support in my challenging journey

Step Change

A quick shout out to a great organisation they were able to give me some sanity and breathing room during my hardest financial times. Your team have been nothing but understanding and supportive and I truly appreciate the value of the service you have provided for me.

Storehouse

Thank you to the Storehouse team and a special thank you also to Natalie. These guys made the difference to me being able to eat regular meals or not. They provided a valuable though underfunded service to those in extreme circumstances. However, more than that they were always there to lend a listening ear and a few words of encouragement regardless of my circumstances. Thanks for the gentle pushes in the right direction and the prayers.

Supernatural

I must also give my thanks to all who work on the hit TV show Supernatural. For those who don't know it is a US show which has been running since 2005 created by Eric Kripke. The storyline features around the relationship between two brothers Sam and Dean who battle a host of supernatural evils. During my dark moments it was one of the few things that brought a little light to my life. The storyline and the characters spoke to me on a deep level and inspired me to keep fighting with a unique combination of action, emotion and humour. It allowed me to see that just because you overcome one trial and another one comes along to slap you in the face you don't give up you just brush yourself off and keep swinging no matter what. I also admire the actors who have reached out to the fans and helped their fans to face their own demons while spreading a little happiness around the world most notably Jared Padalecki with his Keep Fighting Campaign supported by Jensen Ackles and Misha Collins with his Random Acts of Kindness & GISHWHES. Thanks guys you are awesome.

https://www.gishwhes.com/

http://www.randomacts.org/

Bon Jovi

I often used to spend hours sitting alone in my car feeling depressed and alone and I credit the amazing song-writing talent of Bon Jovi for allowing me to wake up one more day. It didn't seem to matter where I was when I was feeling down I would hear one of their songs encouraging me to keep going and not give up, even if I was literally miles from anywhere with the stereo turned off a random car would drive past playing "Keep the Faith". During my recovery I would sing my heart out and it would always bring a smile to my face.

Jon Bon Jovi is also my inspiration for all the work he does for charity including the Jon Bon Jovi Soul Foundation which provides amongst other things the JBJ Soul Kitchen which has served literally thousands of dinners and provides help for people via the Employment Empowerment Team Program which provides a team of professionals to aid in job related skills, financial counselling and legal advice.

One of the greatest moments of my life was being able to touch fingers with Jon Bon Jovi during their concert in Cardiff so thank you for being there with your music for the darkest moments of my life it was truly lifesaving.

http://www.jonbonjovisoulfoundation.org/

And finally to....

The Readers of this book

I hope you enjoyed reading this book and know that I appreciate each and every one of you. Thank you for taking the time to come along on this journey with me. I hope you have found something of value within this book's pages and that it helps you or someone you know to keep taking one step further along the path. Challenges do eventually come to an end so hang in there and I wish you an easier journey from here on out.

Love and Light to you all

Anita x

Printed in Great Britain
by Amazon